With Jesus in
the Upper Room

With Jesus in the Upper Room

A WORKBOOK ON HIS FINAL LESSONS FOR TODAY'S DISCIPLES

MAXIE DUNNAM

 Seedbed

Back cover portrait of Maxie Dunnam by Anthony Thaxton
Cover design by Strange Last Name
Page design by PerfecType, Nashville, Tennessee

Dunnam, Maxie D.
    With Jesus in the Upper Room : a workbook on his final lessons for today's disciples / Maxie Dunnam.
– Frankin, Tennessee : Seedbed Publishing, ©2017.

xiv, 203 pages ; 23 cm. + 1 videodisc

        Includes bibliographical references (pages 201-203)
        ISBN 9781628243970 (paperback : alk. paper)
        ISBN 9781628244014 (DVD)
        ISBN 9781628243987 (mobipocket ebk.)
        ISBN 9781628243994 (epub ebk.)
        ISBN 9781628244007 (updf ebk.)

        1. Bible. John, XIII-XVII–Textbooks. 2. Bible. John, XIII-XVII–Study and teaching. 3. Jesus Chris–Teachings 4. Spiritual exercises. 5. Spiritual formation. I. Title.

BS2616 .D86 2017   226.5

SEEDBED PUBLISHING
Franklin, Tennessee
seedbed.com

CONTENTS

Week Three: Promises, Promises

Week Four: Christ's Chosen People

Week Five: Joy in Relationship with Christ

Week Six: God's Continuing Advocacy

Week Seven: Listening to Jesus Pray

INTRODUCTION

Suppose you had an evening with Jesus—an entire evening—would you listen to Him? Jesus knows that this is the last intimate time He is going to spend with you. He knows He's going to die. What does He need to say? What lessons He has taught you does He need to underscore? How does He need to relate? What actions does He need to take to make clear who He is and what He has tried to communicate?

You don't know what Jesus knows—that He is going to die—but if you did, would you listen?

Chapters 13–17 of John's Gospel is the story of a time like this . . . Jesus' last hours with His closest friends. Passover, the celebration of God's deliverance of His people out of Egyptian captivity, was coming. Jesus knew He had little time before His death, and He wanted to celebrate this monumental event of Passover with those who had become His most faithful followers.

They borrowed an upper room in which to share this evening and a Passover meal. Jesus knew this would be the last supper and the last extended time He would have with them. The disciples didn't know the heaviness of the occasion. From the beginning they were confused, and as the evening went on, they became more perplexed. But before it was over, the deep significance of it all began to settle in their minds and hearts.

John's record of this evening (chapters 13–17) has been called "Jesus' Final Discourse." Some biblical scholars refer to it as "Jesus' Last Will and Testament to His Church." The most precious legacy of Jesus' teaching is here, the distillation of His thought and message— what He really wants us to hear.

Knowing all this, will you listen to Him?

As we give attention to this treasure of Jesus' sharing, we have an advantage even over the disciples who were personally present. Christ is risen and we hear His words from the perspective of promises realized. He has not left us "desolate"; He has come to us (John 14:18). We have experienced His presence and power, so we listen with confidence and assurance. In the next seven weeks, we want to spend some time daily listening to Jesus. We are His modern friends, to whom He speaks as lovingly as He did to His friends in the upper room. My hope and prayer is that we will not simply listen; we will hear, believe, and obey.

I reflect and share these last words of Jesus in a workbook style. I have discovered this to be the most effective way of teaching through writing. It is written to be used, individually or with a group, over a seven-week period.

The Plan

This is a seven-week adventure. It is an individual journey, but my hope is that you will share it with fellow pilgrims who will meet together each week throughout the seven weeks of the study. You are asked to give thirty minutes each day to listen to Jesus. For most people, these thirty minutes will be at the beginning of the day. However, if it is not possible for you to give the time at the beginning of the day, do it whenever the time is available, but do it regularly. The purpose of this spiritual journey must not be forgotten: to incorporate these disciplines into your daily life.

The workbook is arranged in seven major divisions, each designed to guide you for one week. These divisions contain seven sections, one for each day of the week. Each day of the week will have two major aspects: reading the Scripture with commentary, and reflecting and recording.

Reading the Scripture and Commentary

In each day's section you will read Scripture and commentary. Reading Scripture is a basic resource for Christian discipline and living.

Reflecting and Recording

Each day there will be a time for reflecting and recording. This section calls you to record some of your reflections. The degree of meaning you receive from this workbook largely depends on your faithfulness to its practice. You may be unable on a particular day to do precisely what is requested. If so, simply record that fact and make a note of why you couldn't follow through. This may give you insight about yourself and help you to grow, as well.

The emphasis is upon growth, not perfection. Don't feel guilty if you do not follow the pattern of the days exactly. Follow the content and direction seriously but not slavishly. Always remember that this is a personal pilgrimage. What you write in your personal workbook is your private property. You may not wish to share it with anyone. For this reason, no two people should attempt to share the same workbook. The importance of what you write may not mean to someone else what it means to you. Writing, even if it is only brief notes or single-word reminders, helps us clarify our feelings and thinking.

The significance of the reflecting and recording will grow as you move along. Even beyond the seven-week period, you will find meaning in looking back to what you wrote on a particular day in response to a particular situation.

Sharing with Others

You can use this workbook as a private venture without participating in a group. Its meaning will be enhanced, however, if you share the adventure with eight to twelve others. In this way, the priesthood of all believers (see 1 Peter 2:5) will come alive, and you will profit from the growing insights of others, and they will profit from yours. A guide for group sharing is included in the text at the end of each week.

If this is a group venture, all persons should begin their personal involvement with the workbook on the same day, so that when you come together to share as a group all will have been dealing with the same material and will be at the same place in the text. It will be helpful if you have an initial group meeting to get acquainted and to begin the adventure. (Suggested guide to follow.)

Group sessions for this workbook are designed to last ninety minutes (with the exception of this initial meeting). Those sharing in the group should covenant to attend all sessions unless an emergency prevents attendance. Seven weekly sessions will follow this first introductory session.

A group consisting of eight to twelve members is recommended. Larger numbers limit individual involvement. One person can provide the leadership for the entire seven weeks, or leaders can be assigned from week to week. The leader's task: to read directions and determine ahead of time how to handle the session. It may not be possible to use all the suggestions for sharing and praying together. Feel free to select those you think will be most meaningful and those for which you have adequate time. A leader should:

- model a style of openness, honesty, and warmth. A leader should not ask others to share what he or she is not willing to share. Usually the leader should be the first to share, especially as it relates to personal experiences;
- moderate the discussion;
- encourage reluctant members to participate, and try to prevent a few persons from doing all the talking;
- keep the sharing centered in personal experience, rather than academic debate;
- honor the time schedule. If it appears necessary to go longer than ninety minutes, get consensus for continuing another twenty or thirty minutes;
- confirm that meeting time and place are known by all, especially if meetings are held in different homes; and
- make sure necessary materials for meetings are available and that the meeting room is arranged ahead of time. It is desirable that weekly meetings be held in the homes of the participants. (Hosts or hostesses should make sure there are as few interruptions as possible, e.g., children, telephone, pets, etc.). If meetings are held in a church, they should be in an informal setting. Participants are asked to dress casually and to be comfortable and relaxed.

If refreshments are served, they should come after the meeting. In this way, those who wish to stay longer for informal discussion may do so, while those who need to keep to a specific time schedule will be free to leave but will get the full value of the meeting time.

Suggestions for Initial Introductory Meeting

Since the initial meeting is for the purpose of getting acquainted and beginning the shared pilgrimage, here is a way to get started:

- Have each person in the group give his or her full name and the name by which each wishes to be called. Do away with titles. Address all persons by their first name or nickname. Each person should make a list of the names somewhere in his or her workbook. (If name tags are needed, provide them.)
- Let each person in the group share one of the happiest, most exciting, or most meaningful experiences he or she has had during the past three or four weeks. After all participants have shared, lead the group in singing the doxology ("Praise God, from Whom All Blessings Flow") or a familiar chorus of praise.
- After this experience of happy sharing, ask each person who wants to share his or her expectations of the pilgrimage. Why did he or she become a part of it? What does each expect to gain from it? What are their reservations?

The leader should now review the plan for the workbook journey and ask if there are questions about directions and procedures. (This means that the leader should have read the plan prior to the meeting.) If persons have not received copies of the workbook, the books should be made available now. Remember that every person must have his or her own workbook.

Day One in the workbook is the day following this initial meeting, and the next meeting should be held on Day Seven of the first week. If the group must choose another weekly meeting time other than seven days from this initial session, the reading assignment should be brought in harmony with that so that the weekly meetings are always on Day Seven, and Day One is always the day following a weekly meeting.

Nothing binds a group together more than praying for one another.

The leader should encourage each participant to write the names of each person in the group in his or her workbook and commit to praying for them by name daily during this seven weeks.

After checking to see that everyone knows the time and place of the next meeting, the leader may close with a prayer, thanking God for each person in the group, for the opportunity of growth, and for the possibility of growing through listening to Jesus.

Having Loved His Own, He Loved Them to the End

The Holy of Holies of the New Testament

Now before the feast of the Passover, when Jesus knew that his hour had come to depart out of this world to the Father, having loved his own who were in the world, he loved them to the end.

—JOHN 13:1 RSV

What a picture: "having loved his own . . . , he loved them to the end"! With this shimmering description of Jesus, John begins a section of Scripture that has been designated by some scholars as "the Holy of Holies of the New Testament." Chapters 13 through 17, in almost blinding luminosity, reveal the heart of God. The cross is Jesus' most perfect self-revelation in action; these five chapters are His most vivid self-revelation in speech. Gleams of Jesus' heart are unveiled here unlike any other section of Scripture.

Today we are beginning a seven-week reflection/prayer journey with Jesus. We want to look at Him, really look and see. We want to listen, really listen and hear. We want to walk with Him, walk as a friend who wants to garner from the relationship everything that is promised. We want to respond to Him, really respond in loving and joyful obedience.

So let's take our first step. Read again verse one, printed above. Sit quietly for a few minutes and let the Word pervade your mind and heart: "having loved his own . . . , he loved them to the end."

Instead of "to the end" many translators render the verse "unto the uttermost." New Testament scholar E. V. Rieu renders it: "and now he showed how utterly he loved them."[1] Two dynamics are suggested by the different translations. "Unto the uttermost" expresses the depth and degree of Jesus' love; "to the end" suggests the permanence and perpetuity of His love.

Either rendering is staggering to contemplate. We cannot plumb the depth of Christ's love. But also think about this: the dark shadow of the cross, already covering Jesus' life, did not interrupt His love of "his own . . . to the end."

Reflecting and Recording

Spend some time reflecting, and then write a few sentences recording how you feel about Jesus' love for you.

It is incredibly wonderful to know that he loved me and would die for me even if I had been the only sinner in the world. It is even more so to know that he still loves me and cares for me no matter how many times I mess up or let him down. It makes me want to try harder to learn and do what he would want me to do.

During the Day

At mealtimes, pause a moment to offer a prayer of thanksgiving, and affirm, "Jesus loves me, this I know, for the Bible tells me so."

The Passover, "A Piece of Cloth"

The evening meal was in progress, and the devil had already prompted Judas, the son of Simon Iscariot, to betray Jesus. Jesus knew that the Father had put all things under his power, and that he had come from God and was returning to God; so he got up from the meal, took off his outer clothing, and wrapped a towel around his waist. After that, he poured water into a basin and began to wash his disciples' feet, drying them with the towel that was wrapped around him.

—John 13:2–5

Les Misérables is an epic novel that was written by Victor Hugo and published in 1862. It has been cast as a film and also as a musical, long-running on Broadway and theatres across the world. In this masterpiece, Victor Hugo presents a powerful picture of the courage and risks involved in love.

Jean Valjean, the hero in the story, was a kind of Christ figure who, "having loved his own . . . , loved them to the end" (John 13:1 RSV). He loved the little girl, Cosette, and when Cosette's mother died, he assumed the task of parenting her.

Cosette grew up and became a beautiful woman. She fell in love with Marius, who was very possessive of Cosette and distrusted Jean Valjean. He banned Valjean from his house. It was a painful rejection, but Valjean, transparent in his love and extravagant in his self-giving, suffered the estrangement nobly.

Marius was involved in the French Revolution. One night he was wounded at the barricades in the pitch of battle. In spite of the fact that Marius had exiled Valjean from his home and Cosette, Valjean struggled his way through the battle lines, risking his own life, to rescue Marius and to save him for Cosette. He carried Marius on his shoulder through the vast underground sewers of Paris.

The evil Thénardier, a devil figure in the story, was hiding in the sewer. His primary passion was to destroy Valjean. In a struggle with Valjean, Thénardier tore off a piece of Marius's coat. He planned to blackmail Jean Valjean and then send him to the gallows for murdering whom he thought to be the victim on his shoulder.

Jean Valjean, exhausted and near death himself, delivered Marius home, where he recovered and prepared for his wedding to Cosette. In a dramatic scene, Thénardier appeared and confronted Marius with a piece of cloth from the victim's coat, believing that Marius would help him convict the hero. Marius, pale and shaking, went to the closet, picked up his battered and torn coat, matched the piece of cloth with the torn place, and learned for the first time that it had been Valjean who had saved him that night. The man whom he had hated—of whom he had been destructively jealous—had risked his life to save him.

In that moment, Thénardier was unmasked as the scoundrel that he had always been, and Jean Valjean was tearfully reconciled to Marius and restored in love with Cosette.

Can you imagine what that torn piece of cloth meant to Marius? It saved him from estrangement and separation from the man that meant the most to him and to his wife. Can you imagine what that torn piece of coat meant to Jean Valjean? It literally saved his life from return to prison, and even death.

Reflecting and Recording

Our personal memories define who we are. New research and studies have shown that children who have the ability to recall and make sense of memories from daily life can use them to better develop a sense of identity, form relationships, and make sound choices in adolescence and adulthood. Playright James M. Barrie said, "God gave us memory so that we might have roses in December."

The psalmists illustrated the power of memory. They wrote, "tears have been my food" (Ps. 42:3), feeling like "a worm and not a man . . . poured out like water" (Ps. 22:6, 14), "downcast . . . disturbed" (Ps. 43:5); then in the midst of their desolation and moans of despair, they emerged in joyous exaltation. The transition of sadness to joy is captured in words like this: "These things I remember as I pour out my soul: how I used to go to the house of God"(Ps. 42:4) and, "I will remember the deeds of the LORD; yes, I will remember your miracles of long ago" (Ps. 77:11).

Memory is powerful. The psalmists also call upon God to remember: "Remember, LORD, your great mercy and love . . . according to your love remember me, for you, LORD, are good" (Ps. 25:6–7).

We are going to use memory as a spiritual discipline in this journey together. Let's begin by remembering and naming two or three significant events in our lives, with just a brief description to identify the event and/or relationship.

The night my father and I were baptised into the same church. My wedding to Jim. The birth of our son. The time I learned that our son had found his faith in Christ. The birth of our grandson, and his baptism after he had asked Jesus to come into his heart as Savior and Lord.

During the Day

Move through the day especially attentive to things you see, read, or hear that remind you of any of these significant events you have named.

The New Passover

For I received from the Lord what I also delivered to you, that the Lord Jesus on the night when he was betrayed took bread, and when he had given thanks, he broke it, and said, "This is my body which is for you. Do this in remembrance of me." In the same way also the cup, after supper, saying, "This cup is the new covenant in my blood. Do this, as often as you drink it, in remembrance of me." For as often as you eat this bread and drink the cup, you proclaim the Lord's death until he comes.

—1 Corinthians 11:23–26 RSV

Jesus and His disciples gathered in the upper room around "a piece of cloth" that linked them to the most important fact of their faith. The piece of cloth was the Passover. Every year, faithful Jews relived that awesome event in their history when God delivered them from oppressive slavery in Egypt.

God had seen their unbearable horrors and suffering and sent Moses to deliver them. Pharaoh disregarded God's command to let His people go. Even after numerous warnings, and plague after devastating plague, Pharaoh refused to heed God's command.

God shared His plan of deliverance with Moses and Aaron.

The Lord said to Moses and Aaron in Egypt, "This month is to be for you the first month, the first month of your year. Tell the whole community of Israel that on the tenth day of this month each man is to take a lamb for his family, one for each household. If any household is too small for a whole lamb, they must share one with their nearest neighbor, having taken into account the number of people there are. You are to determine the amount of lamb needed in accordance with what each person will eat. The animals you choose must be year-old males without defect, and you may take them from the sheep or the goats. Take care of them until the fourteenth day of the month, when all the members of the community of Israel must slaughter them at twilight. Then they are to take some of the blood and put it on the sides and tops of the doorframes of the houses where they eat the lambs. That same night they are to eat the meat roasted over the fire, along with bitter herbs, and bread made without yeast. Do not eat the meat raw or boiled in water, but roast it over a fire—with the head, legs and internal organs. Do not leave any of it till morning; if some is left till morning, you must burn it. This is how you are to eat it: with your cloak tucked into your belt, your sandals on your feet and your staff in your hand. Eat it in haste; it is the LORD's Passover.

"On that same night I will pass through Egypt and strike down every firstborn of both people and animals, and I will bring judgment on all the gods of Egypt. I am the LORD. The blood will be a sign for you on the houses where you are, and when I see the blood, I will pass over you. No destructive plague will touch you when I strike Egypt.

"This is a day you are to commemorate; for the generations to come you shall celebrate it as a festival to the LORD—a lasting ordinance." (Exod. 12:1–14)

The God who had made covenant with Abraham acted mightily to fulfill that covenant. Jesus and His disciples were celebrating that signal event. Though the disciples didn't know it then, we know now that Jesus was establishing a new covenant, and the next day, He would become the eternal Passover Lamb, sacrificed for our salvation.

In the first days of the church, following Jesus' resurrection and ascension, Christians made this "new Passover" a central act of worship. Read again today's passage from 1 Corinthians. Paul was teaching the Corinthians about the Passover, and the new meaning given by Jesus. Earlier, he said to them: "The cup of blessing which we bless, is it not a participation in the blood of Christ? The bread which we break, is it not a participation in the body of Christ? Because there is one bread, we who are many are one body, for we all partake of the one bread" (1 Cor. 10:16–17 RSV).

So when we Christians come to Holy Communion, we have a torn piece of cloth that tells us of the One who loved us enough to die for us. The bread and the wine are torn from the cross, defining what the cross is all about. In fact, the cross itself is a torn piece of cloth as well—torn from the heart of God. We match this torn piece of cloth with the being of God and discover who He is: "For God so loved the world that he gave his only Son, that whoever believes in him should not perish but have eternal life" (John 3:16 RSV).

What a magnificent description of Jesus: "Having loved his own . . . , he loved them to the end" (John 13:1 RSV). The covenant of God is forever made clear. It is a covenant of love.

Reflecting and Recording

Look back at the events you thought of yesterday in your reflecting and recording time. Do any of them have anything to do with your relationship to Christ? If so, write a few sentences to describe why and how.

My father had been a Christian since childhood, but in a different denomination. His being baptised into the same church on the night I was baptised there on my profession of faith made our family completely united in worship; father, mother and daughter.

During the Day

Find occasions during the day—waiting for an appointment, resting, waiting at a traffic light—to repeat this affirmation: "Having loved his own . . . , he loved them to the end."

Contract and Covenant

"Behold, the days are coming, says the LORD, when I will make a new covenant with the house of Israel and the house of Judah, not like the covenant which I made with their fathers when I took them by the hand to bring them out of the land of Egypt, my covenant which they broke, though I was their husband, says the LORD."

—JEREMIAH 31:31–32 RSV

There are two ways to look at our relationship with God: *contract* and *covenant*.

To see the relationship legalistically, as so many people do, is to think in terms of contract, and to see God as a judge. Though there is law in the Bible, and though God is judge, that's not the dominant image in the Bible. The dominant image is covenant.

One of the ways the meaning of covenant relationship is brought to life is the picture of God as husband. This was Jeremiah's image. Read the above passage again.

Sounds like marriage, doesn't it? And what is a clearer image of covenant than marriage? Marriage is not a contract. When a couple sees it as a contract, the relationship is in trouble. Sure, the state regards marriage as a legal contract, but not the church. The church sees a couple as married not when they *sign* something, but when they *promise* something, when they enter a covenant.

To be sure, the covenant of marriage is fragile, and often broken long before the legal contract of the state is dissolved by divorce. It's fragile, but far more binding in its essence. "I, John, take you, Mary—for better for worse, for richer for poorer, in sickness and in health, to love and to cherish until death separates us."

Fragile words, but a powerful covenant. No fine print, no signing of agreement, just, "I will love you and be faithful."

We can break the covenant—indeed, we do, and our relationship with our spouse is threatened. But here is the good news: we can break our covenant with God, but God, this "husband," will never leave us. "Having loved his own . . . , he loved them to the end" (John 13:1 RSV). Though we separate ourselves from God, reconciliation is always possible. We can always come home.

It's interesting that one way salvation is pictured in the New Testament is as a homecoming. The parable of the prodigal son is a transparent witness of this. When the wayward boy "came to his senses" (Luke 15:17), he knew he needed to be back home. When he returned, the father received him as though he had never been away. He was given a ring, the signet ring of the family, so no one would ever question whether he was a part of the family or not (see Luke 15:11–32).

Reflecting and Recording

Name a covenant you have made; describe it enough to get it firmly in your mind.

Marriage to Jim on Feb. 6, 1964, at First Baptist Church, Memphis, in the chapel, with family and a few friends present.

Name and briefly describe a contract in which you are involved.

The mortgage on our house, which is in both our names, which will finally be paid off in a few months.

What keeps you bound to the covenant you have named? What binds you to the contract?

Love keeps me bound to the covenant: love for my spouse and love for God before whom we made those vows.

Law binds me to the contract, with fear of the legal consequences of being homeless if we do not fulfill it, but also the need to honor a promise.

Spend some time reflecting on your relationship with God. Does it look more like a contract or a covenant? Do you have doubts about God keeping His covenant?

I never doubt God, only myself at times. When I doubt myself, I know that I can ask for forgiveness or guidance or strength, whatever I need, and God will give it. Thanks be to God!

During the Day

Make a copy of this portion of a prayer of St. Patrick. Take it with you today, or put it in a place where you will see it frequently during the day. Pray it as often as you can.

I bind unto myself today:

Christ with me, Christ before me, Christ behind me, Christ within me, Christ beneath me, Christ above me, Christ at my right, Christ at my left, Christ in the heart of everyone who thinks of me, Christ in the mouth of everyone who speaks to me, Christ in every eye that sees me, Christ in every ear that hears me.

I Have Given You an Example

The evening meal was in progress, and the devil had already prompted Judas, the son of Simon Iscariot, to betray Jesus. Jesus knew that the Father had put all things under his power, and that he had come from God and was returning to God; so he got up from the meal, took off his outer clothing, and wrapped a towel around his waist. After that, he poured water into a basin and began to wash his disciples' feet, drying them with the towel that was wrapped around him.

—John 13:2–5

Tony Campollo tells about the Baptist church he attends in the city of Philadelphia. They celebrate a student recognition day once a year on the Sunday between Christmas and New Year's Day. At one service, after six or seven students had spoken, the pastor stood and said, "Children, you are going to die. You may not think you are going to die, but you are. One of these days, they will take you to the cemetery, drop you in a hole, throw some dirt on your face, and go back to the church and eat potato salad." What an opener for a sermon! Shocking.

Jesus' words must have been as shocking, but His actions were even more shocking. He rose from the table, acting like a servant, girded himself with a towel, took a basin of water, and washed all the disciples' feet.

Don't pass over the introductory word to Jesus' dramatic action: "Jesus knew that the Father had put all things under his power, and that he had come from God and was returning to God." Jesus' actions and words came from His knowing who He was.

Friends told me the story of their son who came home from school one day and asked his mother, "Where did I come from?" She was taken aback and said to herself, "Oh, my, here it is!" She and her husband had talked of this day, and sought to prepare themselves for it, so she told him to wait until his father came home and they would discuss it.

Though he knew it would happen sometime, the father was not anxious for the challenge. After dinner, the three of them sat down, and the father and mother hid their nervousness by appearing in control, and with words carefully chosen, explained how human reproduction occurs, and how he was born.

Both parents stammered and perspired a bit, but they made it through, and the father asked, with a kind of sigh, "Now, Tim, does that answer your question?"

Tim, who had listened without a word, responded rather hesitantly, "Yes, and no." "My friend Jimmy said he came from Biloxi, Mississippi."

We can trust the word and action testimony when it comes from someone who knows who he is and where he came from.

The Bible does not tell us when Jesus became aware of who He was, but the message of Scripture is that Jesus was always confident of who He was and why He had come to earth. At the early age of twelve, Jesus was left behind in Jerusalem at the feast of the Passover because His parents supposed that He was in the company of those they were traveling with. After a day's journey, they sought Jesus among their relatives and acquaintances, but couldn't find Him. They returned to Jerusalem.

After three days they found him in the temple courts, sitting among the teachers, listening to them and asking them questions. Everyone who heard him was amazed at his understanding and his answers. When his parents saw him, they were astonished. His mother said to him, "Son, why have you treated us like this? Your father and I have been anxiously searching for you."

"Why were you searching for me?" he asked. "Didn't you know I had to be in my Father's house?"(Luke 2:46–49)

From this account we see that, at the age of twelve, Jesus knew His identity: He was at home in His Father's house.

During His public ministry, He was sure of His identity and calling. When the Pharisees questioned His authority, and sought to know why they should accept His witness and teaching, He told them exactly where He came from: "You are from below; I am from above. You are of this world; I am not of this world" (John 8:23).

Jesus was so confident of His identity that even in the experience of betrayal and facing death, He didn't deny who He was or His calling. In the garden of Gethsemane, he "knelt down and prayed, 'Father, if you are willing, take this cup from me; yet not my will, but yours be done'" (Luke 22:41–42). Jesus knew what He was about to face, and He faced it without wavering.

At His trial, when He refused to respond to the testimony of the Sanhedrin that He had been making claims about being Christ, "[t]he high priest said to him, 'I charge you under oath by the living God: Tell us if you are the Messiah, the Son of God.' [Jesus responded,] 'You have said so'" (Matt. 26:63–64).

He realized that this confession would lead to His eventual death, but He set the record straight. He had no doubts of His identity and calling.

Ponder the way John writes about Him: "Jesus, knowing that the Father had given all things into his hands, and that he had come from God and was going to God, rose from supper, laid aside his garments, and girded himself with a towel" (John 13:3–4 RSV).

Jesus knew who He was: He had come from God, and was going to God.

All sorts of people call us to follow their example. A huge part of television advertising is the personal witness sort, urging us to follow particular examples. The advertisers presume a lot. Why should some television personality know what's the best car for us to drive? Or, why should some bone-crushing athlete have better taste buds and be an authority on either drink or food? Because someone may be stunning and beautiful doesn't mean they have good judgment about mouthwash or toothpaste.

When people are making their testimony, we need to check it out, especially if they are asking us to follow their example. This testimony of Jesus comes from someone who knows who He is, from where He has come, and we can follow that. We can trust the example He offers.

This touched me not only because of my sympathy for the bullied child, but because I know that as long as such attitudes persist, the love for and between ALL people that Jesus taught will not happen.

Reflecting and Recording

Think of a person who has recently shared something with you that got your attention. What did they share? Was it a personal experience? Had they experienced what they talked about? Were they trying to convince you of some conviction of theirs? What about the sharing really got your attention and influenced you to listen?

The person shared something that happened to her child. The child was bullied and accused of telling lies about himself because of his race. I know this child personally and know the accusations were absolutely untrue. Some people cannot be shaken in their opinions by my actions, for less were I to show the opposite truth.

Locate in your memory a Christian witness (testimony) that impacted your life. Make enough notes about that experience to get it firmly in mind.

A visiting preacher from Australia, during a revival, told the details of his own conversion experience during World War II. It was this story that woke me up to my own need to make a commitment to Christ.

Looking back on that experience, what made you think the witness was worth listening to? *He told of how he had lived before and it was clear that Jesus had changed his life.*

During the Day

Seek at least one opportunity today to share your faith with someone. Flavor that witness with "knowing who you are, and from where you have come."

Power That Stoops to Serve

A dispute also arose among them as to which of them was considered to be greatest. Jesus said to them, "The kings of the Gentiles lord it over them; and those who exercise authority over them call themselves Benefactors. But you are not to be like that. Instead, the greatest among you should be like the youngest, and the one who rules like the one who serves. For who is greater, the one who is at the table or the one who serves? Is it not the one who is at the table? But I am among you as one who serves."

—LUKE 22:24–27

Luke tells the story of the dispute among the disciples about who was greatest in the context of Jesus' last supper as they celebrated Passover together. Luke, however, does not tell of the foot washing. Yet, he provides a sentence that finds its true meaning in Jesus' act of foot washing: "But I am among you as one who serves" (v. 27).

The foot washing was the signal act in the event. This is clear in the way John, in introducing the story, records Jesus' reason for doing what He did. These reasons are stated in two convictions of Jesus, which have an intimate connection with Jesus' call to a foot-washing style of life.

John 13:1 expresses one of those convictions: "[W]hen Jesus knew that his hour had come to depart out of this world to the Father, having loved his own who were in the world, he loved them to the end" (RSV). His loving them *to the end,* not just to the end of His life, but loving them "to the uttermost," required that He share as clearly as possible who He was and the life to which He was calling them.

The second conviction that leads to His act of foot washing is stated: "Jesus knew that the Father had put all things under his power, and that he had come from God and was returning to God; so he got up from the meal, took off his outer clothing, and wrapped a towel around his waist" (John 13:3–4). Jesus was absolutely conscious of His divine nature, and this led Him to perform this act of a slave. He who was so high stooped so low. Loftiness was joined with lowliness to demonstrate a love that serves.

The humble know who they are. Albert Schweitzer was once working around the hospital in Lambaréné, when a visitor from America saw him pushing a wheelbarrow. He was shocked that this renowned doctor would stoop to such manual labor, so he asked, "How is it, Doctor, that you push a wheelbarrow?" Without stopping, Dr. Schweitzer replied, "With two hands."

Reflecting and Recording

Recall here some act you performed or some relationship you shared that would come closest to a foot-washing style.

I have been the family caretaker wherever there was need. I believe this was my gift from God, to be able to do this. Having to be the one taken care of gave me a new perspective on the other side of that experience.

Spend a few minutes reflecting on your daily life. How close does it come to a foot-washing style? *Some days are better than others.*

During the Day

Seek a specific opportunity today to stoop and serve.

The Nature of Humility

Jesus knew that the Father had put all things under his power, and that he had come from God and was returning to God; so he got up from the meal, took off his outer clothing, and wrapped a towel around his waist. After that, he poured water into a basin and began to wash his disciples' feet, drying them with the towel that was wrapped around him.

He came to Simon Peter, who said to him, "Lord, are you going to wash my feet?"

Jesus replied, "You do not realize now what I am doing, but later you will understand."

"No," said Peter, "you shall never wash my feet."

Jesus answered, "Unless I wash you, you have no part with me."

"Then, Lord," Simon Peter replied, "not just my feet but my hands and my head as well!"

Jesus answered, "Those who have had a bath need only to wash their feet; their whole body is clean. And you are clean, though not every one of you." For he knew who was going to betray him, and that was why he said not every one was clean.

—John 13:3–11

There is true humility and there is affected humility. Look at the contrast between Jesus and Peter. When Jesus came to Peter to wash his feet, Peter resisted: "Lord, do not wash my feet" (author's paraphrase). I'm sure there was real sincerity in that. But sincerity and humility are not the same.

Peter was struggling in his relationship with Jesus, struggling with his own life, struggling with what was going on because things were not turning out as he thought they might when he left his fishing boat and followed this itinerant preacher. And he certainly didn't understand what Jesus was doing. He couldn't understand why Jesus was deliberately taking the position of a servant, so he *acted* humbly and backed away from Jesus because he didn't want his leader washing his feet. It was a kind of affected humility.

But not the humility expressed by Jesus. As I said yesterday, the humble know who they are. Jesus knew who He was; Peter did not yet know who he was.

In our culture, it is easy to have distorted notions about humility. We think of it as a kind of cowering, taking a backseat kind of style. In our most mistaken notions, we stereotype the humble person as being without strength, allowing people to take advantage of them, and staying in the shadow. That's not true humility.

A father made this confession. Every night he would bring work home from the office; lots of work, work he would begin doing right after the evening meal. One night his son asked him why he brought all this work home. He explained, probably too adult-like, that he was a very busy person, his job was demanding, and he just had more work to do than he could get done at the office.

I like what the little boy said. From his world, and the way they did it at school, he asked, "Well, in that case, why don't they put you in a slower group?"

Is anything more needed—to know who we are and, thus, to be genuinely humble? This means knowing our weaknesses, as well as our strengths. Perhaps more than anything else the humble not only know they are vulnerable, they know their Source of power. They live from the inside out, not the outside in. The humble have power, but the power is not so much in them as through them.

I'm not a baseball fan, but I relish sports stories of perspective and power, of humility and greatness. One of my favorite stories speaks to this issue of humility, of living from the inside out, not the outside in.

After the Dodgers won the Pennant in 1988, they gave their star pitcher, Orel Hershiser, a three-year contract for 7.7 million dollars. Though I have real problems with that sort of price tag on sports stars, it does say that Hershiser was a phenomenal player.

In Game Two of that series, Hershiser was pitching. He got two doubles and a single at bat, as many hits and more total bases than he allowed the competing team. He ran the bases like Jackie Robinson, and shut out Oakland 6–0.

Then came the fifth and final game. Folks wondered if Hershiser was going to make it again. He had to talk his manager into letting him stay in when he got into trouble in the eighth inning. He went on to win the series by winning that final game 5–2.

What fans remembered for a long time, though, was watching Hershiser on television on the bench in the top half of an inning, leaning back, mouth wide open, singing to himself that last night. It wasn't until later on that we learned exactly what he was doing. He was singing to himself two songs: The Doxology—"Praise God from whom all blessings flow . . ."—and a contemporary Christian tune by the late Keith Green called "Rushing Wind." A line in that song goes: "Rushing wind, blow through this temple, blowing out the dust within."[1]

Hershiser said he wanted to cleanse his mind of all the clutter of the world in that moment, to block out the pressure, and concentrate on the game at hand. This was a convincing picture of living from the inside out, not the outside in.

As with Jesus, so with Hershiser and us, when we know who we are, we know our Source of power.

Reflecting and Recording

Did you follow through with yesterday's suggestion to seek a specific opportunity to stoop and serve? Make some notes, honestly expressing your feelings about that exercise.

Other than the usual household chores, which I thank God for restoring me to be able to perform, I didn't really find any specific opportunity.

I did give away something that I had bought by mistake when I thought it was something else to a place where it was needed, but that was less from a desire to do good as from a desire to have the thing gone. Knowing it helped someone else was just an extra.

What does it mean to live from the inside out, rather than the outside in? Can you think of incidents when you expressed that kind of living?

Focusing on knowing who you are and where you are rather than letting outside circumstances influence how you think of yourself and how you act as a result.

During the Day

Find an occasion today to talk to someone about what it means to live from the inside out. Maybe tell them the story of Hershiser to get the discussion going.

GROUP MEETING FOR WEEK ONE

• INTRODUCTION •

These group sessions will be meaningful to the degree that they reflect the experience of all participants. The guide is simply an effort to facilitate personal sharing. Therefore, do not be rigid in following these suggestions. Leaders, especially, should seek to be sensitive to what is going on in the lives of the participants and to focus on the group sharing of these experiences.

Ideas are important. We should wrestle with new ideas as well as ideas with which we disagree. It is important, however, that the group meeting not become a debate about ideas. The emphasis should be upon persons, shared experiences, and relationships. Content is important—but how content applies to our individual lives and our relationship to Christ is most important.

As the group comes to the place where all can share honestly and openly, the more meaningful the experience will be. This does not mean sharing only the good or positive; but also the questions, struggles, difficulties, and the negatives.

The process is not easy; it is deceptive to pretend it is. Growth requires effort. Don't be afraid to share your questions, reservations, and dry periods, as well as that in which you find meaning.

• SHARING TOGETHER •

1. Leaders, begin the group with prayer. Then, if necessary, invite each person to introduce him or herself, giving their full name and the name by which they wish to be called.
2. Invite each person to share the most meaningful day with the workbook this week, beginning with the leader.

3. Invite those who are willing to share their most difficult day, and why it was difficult.

4. Invite two or three persons to share the occasion when they accepted the fact that they were truly loved by God.

5. (Leaders, be sensitive to time; remember the meeting is scheduled to last no more than ninety minutes.) Spend five to ten minutes discussing the difference between a relationship being a covenant or a contract.

6. Leaders, be sure to save at least five minutes for closing prayer time. With the time you have left, invite participants to share their memory of a Christian witness (testimony) that impacted their life.

• PRAYING TOGETHER •

Suggestions for this time will be offered each week. The leader should examine these ahead of time—regarding them only as suggestions. What is happening in the meeting—the mood, the needs that are expressed, the timing—should determine the direction of the group's praying together.

Leaders should introduce the prayer time with something like this:

Corporate prayer is one of the great blessings of Christian community, but that prayer does not always have to be verbal. In this time of prayer we are going to be praying silently. I hope you have written the name of each person in your group somewhere in your workbook. Look at that list now. Let's spend about three minutes going through our lists. As you see a name, think of what that person has shared in this session, and simply breathe a prayer, "Lord, I offer up [fill in the blank] to You for Your blessing."

After sufficient time, invite the group to join you in praying together the Lord's Prayer.

A Foot-Washing Style of Life

More Than an Example

When he had finished washing their feet, he put on his clothes and returned to his place. "Do you understand what I have done for you?" he asked them. "You call me 'Teacher' and 'Lord,' and rightly so, for that is what I am. Now that I, your Lord and Teacher, have washed your feet, you also should wash one another's feet. I have set you an example that you should do as I have done for you. Very truly I tell you, no servant is greater than his master, nor is a messenger greater than the one who sent him. Now that you know these things, you will be blessed if you do them."

—John 13:12–17

On Day Seven of last week we looked at Peter's response to Jesus' effort to wash his feet. Peter resisted. Surely, he was sincere in that, but as I noted on Day Six, sincerity and humility are not the same.

Peter was struggling in his relationship with Jesus and with what was going on, no doubt confused and wondering why he had left his fishing boat and followed this itinerant preacher. Now, he certainly didn't understand what Jesus was doing, when Jesus told him that if he did not let Him wash his feet, "you have no part with me" (John 13:8).

How characteristic of Peter—never shy or timid, never holding back, and often without thinking, speaking whatever he was feeling: "'Then, Lord,' Simon Peter replied, 'not just my feet but my hands and my head as well!'" (v. 9). If this foot washing means receiving all the benefits of Christ, then why not wash my whole body? The more washing, the better!

He missed it completely. He didn't, perhaps he couldn't, understand that Jesus was deliberately taking the position of a servant to demonstrate His own true nature and the nature of His call to those who would follow. It is the foot washing that is important because "I have set you an example that you should do as I have done for you" (v. 15).

Jesus is calling us to a foot-washing lifestyle. He is rather clear: "'Now that I, your Lord and Teacher, have washed your feet, you also should wash one another's feet. I have set you an example that you should do as I have done for you'" (vv. 14–15). The act is more dramatic from a distance. Unlike the disciples, who had not yet experienced the resurrection, we know who this is. The foot-washing person here is the One who from the beginning was "with God, and the Word was God" (John 1:1). This is the Lord who nullified the sting of death and was Victor over the grave. This is the One who, after appearing to His disciples alive after His resurrection, ascended into heaven, where He reigns at the right hand of the Father.

How can it be? Our awesome God, washing the grimy feet of His followers?

Reflecting and Recording

When you think about Jesus, what actions of His come immediately to your mind? List some of those.

Healing the sick and the disabled, forgiving the woman caught in adultery, throwing out the ones dishonoring the temple, casting out demons, weeping over Jerusalem, praying for his disciples and future ones.

If you listed foot washing, my hunch is that you did so only because we have been focusing on this particular event. Yet, I believe that most readers would see Jesus as the personification of humility. That you would normally not list foot washing as an action that characterized Jesus' ministry makes the point that Jesus was using this as an example. The point He was making was not that when His followers come together they should wash each other's feet; rather, they are to live together in a foot-washing style of life, mutually caring for one another. But more important, serving is to be their style of daily life.

Name two people you know whom you believe demonstrate a serving lifestyle.

Drew Sippel
Nicklaus Carter

During the Day

Call or write those two people a note, thanking them for their serving lifestyle.

A Parable in Action

When he had finished washing their feet, he put on his clothes and returned to his place. "Do you understand what I have done for you?" he asked them. "You call me 'Teacher' and 'Lord,' and rightly so, for that is what I am. Now that I, your Lord and Teacher, have washed your feet, you also should wash one another's feet. I have set you an example that you should do as I have done for you."

—JOHN 13:12–15

Jesus washing His disciples' feet is an incredible act—voluntarily doing the menial work of a slave. On Day Seven of last week, we focused on Peter drawing back in embarrassed pride, emphatically refusing to accept this flabbergasting gesture of grace. Most of us can empathize with Peter because we are a lot like him. How can I—a weak, sinful, stubborn person—accept this outpouring of grace?

But there is more to the story here than shock over Jesus' actions and our feelings of unworthiness. The problem is deeper. We are great achievers. We work our way up. We live under the delusion that we are in control and we can make it on our own. So having one kneel before us in a humble act of service challenges our well-practiced self-perception of independence and strength.

Look explicitly at the example Jesus gave. What had He done? He had washed His disciples' feet. Did this mean that every time the disciples got together one of them should wash the rest of their feet? No. This was a parable in action.

Jesus went immediately from giving the example to talking about what it means to be a servant. So, Jesus was giving this example of being a servant to sound His call.

My preacher friend, Donald Shelby, once told me this story of a young soldier in a field hospital, dying of wounds sustained on the front lines. A chaplain came to his side. "Will you write a letter to my mother?" asked the young man. "Tell her that I died happy. And will you also write my Sunday school teacher? Her name and address are somewhere in my wallet. Tell her I died a Christian."

The chaplain honored the soldier's request. In a couple of weeks a reply came from the Sunday school teacher which read: "I can't tell you what your letter meant to me, and how moved I am by Richard's remembering me. I'm still teaching the junior high class in my church, but lately I had become discouraged and was ready to quit. After your letter came, I decided to continue. There may be another young Richard in the class who may find his way to the Lord. By God's grace, I'll endure."

It's a challenging picture of servanthood. If you and I are to follow Jesus' example, we must forget ourselves in concern for others. We must take the risks of love. We must care enough to give ourselves and keep on giving ourselves. We must even care enough for rowdy junior high boys, to meet with them in a Sunday school class week after week.

Reflecting and Recording

Think of those two persons you named yesterday as models of a serving lifestyle. Name them again as an affirmation of gratitude.

Drew Sippel

Nicholaus Carter

As you think of them, how did they forget themselves in serving? Did they take risks in loving? How? In what ways did they give themselves and their time?

Drew went into areas where he was in many minds unwanted, certainly unappreciated, his intentions, motives and methods questioned, to make education, self-belief and hope for a better life available to children who needed it. Nick, a teenager, not only by joining service groups at church and school, but by simply opening his loving heart to those around him and going out of his way to be a friend and meet needs where he saw them, was and

willing to meet similar doubts and misunderstandings to live and love like Jesus.

What do you see in them that you most need to add to your life if you are going to be a servant?

Courage, energy, caring and willingness to take risks.

During the Day

Deliberately seek to practice some of what you need to add to your life from the inspiration of the servant persons you have been considering.

Self-Affirmation and Self-Depreciation

Jesus knew that the Father had put all things under his power, and that he had come from God and was returning to God; so he got up from the meal . . . wrapped a towel around his waist . . . and began to wash his disciples' feet . . .

—John 13:3–5

Then he said to them all: "Whoever wants to be my disciple must deny themselves and take up their cross daily and follow me. For whoever wants to save their life will lose it, but whoever loses their life for me will save it. What good is it for someone to gain the whole world, and yet lose or forfeit their very self?"

—Luke 9:23–25

We don't reflect enough upon what serving could do for our sense of identity, our need for strong self-expression and self-affirmation. When we become servants after the style of Jesus, we decide what kind of person we are going to be. We steel ourselves against being shaped into the image of the faceless crowd of a world that is driven to conform, to get and spend and consume and die without impacting anything except the gross national product.

To be a servant after the style of Jesus is to gain an identity, not to lose it. Remember what I said earlier. The humble know who they are. I know the arguments of those who disparage Jesus' call to deny ourselves. They have distorted those words with the false perspective that Jesus was encouraging self-abnegation, self-disparagement, and self-depreciation. Such interpreters have indicted Jesus for adding to people's emotional

35

problems and creating troubled personalities through neurotic repression and distortion of authentic assertion and confidence. How wrong such understandings are.

Jesus' call to self-denial means precisely the opposite of self-depreciation. He is bidding us to become the persons God created us to be. So, rather than contributing to a sense of inferiority and self-doubt that plagues so many people, causing them to feel unworthy and unloved, Jesus gives us a purpose and a direction for life that underscores meaning. What could give us more identity, a greater portion of self-worth, a more pronounced sense of purpose, than to know ourselves to be a channel through whom God can love the world, can give grace and hope to the world, can bring light to dark places, and beauty to ugliness? That's precisely who we become when we become servants for Christ's sake—agents of God, channels through which His love is manifest in the world.

Reflecting and Recording

The last paragraph makes some bold claims about how following Jesus as servants gives us identity and a pronounced sense of purpose as we become the channels through which God can do His work. In a few sentences, describe how you can fulfill these claims of God acting through you in the space provided below.

God can love the world

When I show love to those I encounter

God can give grace and hope to the world

When I act to make someone's life better and, if asked, share that it is because of God's love that I do it.

God can bring light to dark places and beauty to ugliness

When I contribute in some way, by word, prayer, action or finances, toward seeing these things done.

During the Day

In some way, no matter how simple, be a channel for God to act as you have described above.

The Church as Servant

Jesus spoke to them again in parables, saying: "The kingdom of heaven is like a king who prepared a wedding banquet for his son. He sent his servants to those who had been invited to the banquet to tell them to come, but they refused to come.

"Then he sent some more servants and said, 'Tell those who have been invited that I have prepared my dinner: My oxen and fattened cattle have been butchered, and everything is ready. Come to the wedding banquet.'

"But they paid no attention and went off—one to his field, another to his business. The rest seized his servants, mistreated them and killed them. The king was enraged. He sent his army and destroyed those murderers and burned their city.

"Then he said to his servants, 'The wedding banquet is ready, but those I invited did not deserve to come. So go to the street corners and invite to the banquet anyone you find.' So the servants went out into the streets and gathered all the people they could find, the bad as well as the good, and the wedding hall was filled with guests."

—Matthew 22:1–10

For three days, we have looked at the call to servanthood from a personal perspective. Let's now consider the call and the example from the perspective of the church, as an expression of the kingdom.

Jesus' parable of the kingdom, in which He likened the kingdom to a marriage feast, is our focus. Have you ever noticed the fact that Jesus not only went to parties, He talked a lot about them? It's interesting to stop and consider how many of His parables include a party. The parable of the five wise and the five foolish virgins is built around a wedding party. In another parable, a woman loses a coin, and when she finds it, she calls her neighbors and says, "Let's celebrate." And, perhaps the most famous one, the story of the prodigal son, ends with a party—with a father, his family, and all of the servants making merry because a lost son has come home.

In the parable we consider today, Jesus said the kingdom of heaven could be compared to a king who gave a marriage feast for his son. When it looked as though no one was coming to the party, the king was disappointed; no one was accepting his invitation. So he sent his servants out to those who had been invited and tried to convince them to come. "Come on, the table is spread, the party is ready!" But those who had been invited made light of the invitation, offered ridiculous excuses, and refused to come.

This made the king angry. He ordered his troops to destroy people who had been invited and to burn their city. But, he didn't forget the party. The party had to go on, so he sent his servants out into the streets and the alleyways of the city to find as many people as they could find, and bring them in.

The servants went everywhere—into the center city as well as into the suburbs. On the wrong side as well as on the right side of the track; into every ethnic enclave; among the impoverished, as well as among the rich. Soon the wedding hall was filled with people and the king was able to celebrate his son's wedding.

Jesus was telling the story for a very specific purpose, the people to whom He was talking needed to hear that God had first invited into His kingdom a chosen people, the Jews, but they had not responded. They made ridiculous excuses—they even persecuted and killed the prophets. So, since those originally invited wouldn't accept the invitation, God finally sent His messengers out into the world's unlikely highways and everybody was invited to come in, including, especially, the Gentiles. That's the primary meaning of the parable.

Accepting that point, look at the crowd that came to the party. It must have been a motley crew—all elements of society, from every walk of life. And Jesus says, "That's what the kingdom is going to be like, and that's what the church should represent."

I doubt if anyone has understood this more in modern times than Gen. William Booth, founder of the Salvation Army. The American poet Vachel Lindsey, in his poem "General William Booth Enters into Heaven," pictured William Booth entering heaven and the procession following in this way:

Walking lepers followed, rank on rank,

Lurching bravoes from the ditches dank,

Drabs from the alleyways and drug fiends pale—

Minds still passion-ridden, soul-powers frail:—

Vermin-eaten saints with mouldy breath,

Unwashed legions with the ways of Death—

That's a dramatic description of those who are going to stumble into the king's great celebration when the last trumpet is sounded and the kingdom is established.

There are two questions the church must ask herself: Who are the persons not like us who should receive a first invitation from us? Are we willing to go out into the city and compel the unlikely to come to the party?

Reflecting and Recording

Spend some time reflecting on the two questions the church must ask herself. Is there a particular group in your community that would be considered unlikely to come to the party?

Probably the LGBT groups, activists and people with same-sex partners, with or without civil marriage.

If your church decided to invite them, make some notes about what you might do in relation to them, and how you would extend the invitation.

I would probably not be the one who would be in a position to do the inviting. If they came and I knew who they were, the most I could do would be to say "Good morning, glad you came" the way I would to anyone else.

During the Day

If you are sharing this journey with a group of people, identify one of those persons with whom you are going to speak today about your congregation extending an invitation. Discuss whether you have identified the same people and how you might extend the invitation to them.

DAY FIVE

Is It I?

"I am not referring to all of you; I know those I have chosen. But this is to fulfill this passage of Scripture: 'He who shared my bread has turned against me.'

"I am telling you now before it happens, so that when it does happen you will believe that I am who I am. Very truly I tell you, whoever accepts anyone I send accepts me; and whoever accepts me accepts the one who sent me."

After he had said this, Jesus was troubled in spirit and testified, "Very truly I tell you, one of you is going to betray me."

His disciples stared at one another, at a loss to know which of them he meant. One of them, the disciple whom Jesus loved, was reclining next to him. Simon Peter motioned to this disciple and said, "Ask him which one he means."

Leaning back against Jesus, he asked him, "Lord, who is it?"

Jesus answered, "It is the one to whom I will give this piece of bread when I have dipped it in the dish." Then, dipping the piece of bread, he gave it to Judas, the son of Simon Iscariot. As soon as Judas took the bread, Satan entered into him.

So Jesus told him, "What you are about to do, do quickly." But no one at the meal understood why Jesus said this to him. Since Judas had charge of the money, some thought Jesus was telling him to buy what was needed for the festival, or to give something to the poor. As soon as Judas had taken the bread, he went out. And it was night.

—John 13:18–30

Jesus had no trouble getting the attention of those to whom He spoke. His words often exploded an emotional bomb in their minds. It was certainly the case in our Scripture. "One of you is going to betray me" (v. 21). Bang! That got their attention. No doubt it was an explosive thought in each of their minds and they began to search their hearts.

But that's not the only bomb He set off that evening. A second bomb was detonated in the personal encounter He had with Peter. We didn't read it in our Scripture lesson. The story is that Judas went out into the night and Jesus continued to talk about what was going to happen to Him. "I am with you for a little while," He said, "but I am going to leave . . . and where I am going you cannot come" (John 13:33, author's paraphrase).

Well, you can imagine what a mysterious and shocking word that was. Peter, always aggressive and assertive in his relationship with the Lord, was the one who raised the question, "Where are you going?"

Again, Jesus reiterated, "Where I am going you cannot follow me now, but you will follow later" (v. 36).

Well, that was just as puzzling, so Peter pressed Him: "Lord, why can't I follow you now? I will lay down my life for you" (v. 37).

Then came the bombshell. "You'd lay down your life for me, Peter? Ah, no. What is going to happen is that before the cock crows, you are going to betray me three times" (v. 38, author's paraphrase).

Judas and Peter—folks like us—betrayal and denial—bombshells. None of us are exempt from the possibility of spiritual and moral failure. Not many months pass without news about some outstanding public figure falling. The more famous they are, the more news they get. And religious leaders are not exempt.

I remember an occasion when media was full of the moral failures of three well-known religious leaders. I had been invited to participate in a group of twenty-five to dialogue about church growth and leadership. We were going to be led by an outstanding leader, a person who had written a number of popular books. Because the press was filled with the stories of the failures of other religious leaders, he felt compelled to share with our convenor the fact that he was having difficulty following through on his commitment to us. He had had an affair that few people knew about, but it could become public. The affair was long past and his marriage seemed secure. The convenor polled our group; he wanted to know if we wished to withdraw our invitation to this fellow because of his moral and spiritual failure.

I voted not to withdraw the invitation because none of us are exempt from the possibility of moral and spiritual failure; the man was honest in sharing and his marital relationship seemed to be intact.

Correct theology doesn't provide ultimate protection. A big part of history is the story of the fall of great men. Think of King David. Scripture calls him "a man after [God's] own heart" (Acts 13:22). The hero of Israel, the singer of God's songs of praise and trust and confidence. But listen to him as he moans and groans in one of those songs.

> Have mercy on me, O God, according to your unfailing love; according to great compassion blot out my transgressions. Wash away all my iniquity and cleanse me from my sin.
>
> For I know my transgressions, and my sin is always before me. Against you, you only, have I sinned and done what is evil in your sight . . . (Ps. 51:1–4)

None of us are exempt. Judas and Peter warned us against the sin of pride and over-confidence. Judas thought he knew best. Peter thought his strength of commitment would sustain him. Outright betrayal is probably not a part of our experience—but denial? Hardly a day passes, for most of us, when we do not deny or betray in one way or another. In its most common expression, denial comes in our failure to live out our discipleship, to be faithful in following Jesus.

In the Emmaus movement, we have what are called reunion groups—small groups of people who gather weekly or biweekly to share their Christian walk with one another. The purpose of these groups is to hold each other accountable and to remind each other of our call to discipleship. In the reunion group, we talk about the occasions during the week when we have felt closest to Christ. That's always a strength-giving time of sharing. But we also examine ourselves for failure. We ask ourselves the questions: When did I have the opportunity to share Christ, to witness, but failed to do so? When did I fail in relationship to others—to love, to care, to understand, to listen, to support? Did I stand by when someone maligned the character of another? Did I fail to lend my moral weight to a cause of righteousness?

It's a spiritual discipline called *examination of conscience*. It's an effective disciple-growth practice, and a sure way to guard against betrayal and denial.

Reflecting and Recording

When was the most recent occasion that you were most powerfully tempted to or actually did deny or betray Him? Get that experience firmly in your mind.

A person I love deeply has never accepted Christ. Whenever I have tried to discuss that, I am told to drop it or that one will have no more to do with me. In fear of losing that relationship, I back down.

Make some brief notes about how you escaped the temptation to deny or betray. If you thought of an actual betrayal experience, briefly describe how you have dealt with that experience.

I try to rationalize backing down by telling myself that without the relationship I will have no chance to demonstrate Christian living and perhaps win that way. I have on rare occasions spoken up briefly and in a way that is non-threatening to that one's persona, but I let too many chances pass without saying anything. I pray regularly for forgiveness and courage.

During the Day

The end of the day is a good time for an examination of conscience. If you are not presently doing so, begin that practice today. The following are some good questions to help you begin that practice: Did I fail to share Christ today when I had a clear opportunity to speak or act? Was there a failure to love and care in a relationship? Did I remain silent when someone's character was maligned? Did I shade the truth or deliberately communicate a falsehood? Did I fail to lend my moral weight to a cause of righteousness?

Will You Lay Down Your Life for Me?

When he was gone, Jesus said, "Now the Son of Man is glorified and God is glorified in him. If God is glorified in him, God will glorify the Son in himself, and will glorify him at once.

"My children, I will be with you only a little longer. You will look for me, and just as I told the Jews, so I tell you now: Where I am going, you cannot come.

"A new command I give you: Love one another. As I have loved you, so you must love one another. By this everyone will know that you are my disciples, if you love one another."

Simon Peter asked him, "Lord, where are you going?"

Jesus replied, "Where I am going, you cannot follow now, but you will follow later."

Peter asked, "Lord, why can't I follow you now? I will lay down my life for you."

Then Jesus answered, "Will you really lay down your life for me? Very truly I tell you, before the rooster crows, you will disown me three times!"

—John 13:31–38

There is a little church on the Appian Way, not far from Rome, that bears the interesting name *The Church of the Quo Vadis*. Those Latin words, *Quo Vadis*, mean "Whither goest thou?" Legend has it that a few years after the crucifixion of Jesus, Peter had been in Rome and was under the threat of persecution. He was fleeing for his life—leaving the city in fear—when he met Jesus. Jesus was headed into the city, so Peter asked Him the question, "Lord, whither goes thou?" And the Master answered, "I go to Rome, to be crucified again." The answer so pierced Peter's mind and heart that it turned this cowardly fugitive into a hero, and he followed his Lord back into Rome, where he gladly died. Peter was crucified upside down on a cross, at his own request, because he felt that he was not worthy to die as the Lord.

Though a legend, the church is there to tell a moving story. I share it because the question that Peter asked the Lord in that story is the same question he asked Him in our Scripture lesson. Peter didn't understand.

All the characteristics of this fascinating personality, Simon Peter, are in operation. Reading the Scripture attentively, you will notice that Peter has broken in upon Christ's solemn words, entirely deaf to their meaning. He lays hold of one thought, that Jesus is departing, and that he is to be left alone. So he asks the question, "Lord, where are you going?" What he really means is, "Tell me where, and then I will come too."

Jesus knew all Peter was thinking, so He continues the conversation by laying that hard word on Peter: "Will you really lay down your life for me?" (John 13:38). Could there be a tougher question? It not only pierces the shallow thinking of Peter, it is the commitment question for us as well.

Today and tomorrow, let's come at the question a step at a time in order to capture the full meaning of it, and struggle with integrity for an answer. In my struggle with it, I've shaped three other questions. As we answer these questions, we will be responding to Jesus, as He asks us the question He asked Peter.

Isn't Jesus asking, Will you make My will your will? That will help us get at the more piercing commitment question, Will you lay down your life for Me?

Dr. Carl Barth was one of the premier theologians of the twentieth century. I believe it was Dr. Paul Tillich, another eminent theologian who, commenting on this great and controversial thinker, said that Dr. Barth refused to become his own follower.

He pointed out that Barth had changed his mind about some things from time to time, but that he steadfastly refused to take himself so seriously that he would deliberately establish a school of thought.

He refused to become his own follower. Isn't that our temptation—*to become our own follower*—to do our own will—to go our self-centered way without respect to any ultimate demands that might be made upon us? "Will you make My will your will?"

In his book *Who Is Jesus?*, Bruce Demarest told of a visit he once had with Mahatma Gandhi. After a time, the conversation turned to spiritual matters. He tactfully related to Gandhi his own personal experience of Christ being Lord and occupying the throne of his life. Gandhi quietly thought for a moment and then lamented, "My own throne is still vacant."[1]

That's a very sad sentence, isn't it? But the sadder picture is that each one of us is sitting on the throne of our own life. Most of us know that the throne of our life is not vacant. We sit there. We seek to be the masters of our fate and the captains of our souls.

Christ is not going to take the throne of our life because we happen to leave it vacant, and He certainly will not take it by storm. If He gets it, it will be because we give it to Him by deliberate, conscious, willing choice.

Reflecting and Recording

Read slowly and reflectively the last paragraph above, then rewrite it here in your own words and way of expression.

God made a way for us to have a relationship with him, to know truth and to have a good life, but he also gave us free will. He won't force us to take his way; the choice is ours. If we make the wrong choice, we sadden God's heart, but we are the real losers.

During the Day

As suggested yesterday, close today with an examination of conscience. Here are the questions again for your guidance. Did I fail to share Christ today when I had a clear opportunity to speak or act? Was there a failure to love and care in a relationship? Did I remain silent when someone's character was maligned? Did I shade the truth or deliberately communicate a falsehood? Did I fail to lend my moral weight to a cause of righteousness?

Style and Power

Simon Peter asked him, "Lord, where are you going?"
Jesus replied, "Where I am going, you cannot follow now, but you will follow later."
Peter asked, "Lord, why can't I follow you now? I will lay down my life for you."
Then Jesus answered, "Will you really lay down your life for me? Very truly I tell you, before the rooster crows, you will disown me three times!"

—John 13:36–38

We are seeking to deal with this question of Jesus a step at a time by posing questions integral to this piercing one: "Will you really lay down your life for me?" (v. 38). Jesus asked Peter that question when blustering Peter had rushed ahead in the conversation, by asking, "Lord, why can't I follow you now?" Then without waiting for an answer, he boasts, "I will lay down my life for you" (v. 37). Knowing Peter doesn't know what he is talking about, Jesus turns Peter's rash boast into the piercing question, "Will you really lay down your life for me?"

Yesterday we considered a lesser emotionally impactful expression of Jesus' question that might help us answer Jesus with integrity: Will you make My will your will? Following that pattern, consider this question: Will you make My style your style?

We've talked about this in terms of foot washing as a metaphor for servant. Think about it a bit more. While we often talk about Jesus turning the world upside down, it may be more accurate to say that He showed us that we live in an upside-down world. Jesus slashed at the Pharisees, the very best of the Jewish community when he said blessed are the meek, the hungry, and the poor. In Jericho, He turned His back on the leading citizens and stayed with the social outcast, a tax collector. He held as valued by God those whom the world despises. He showed us, that alongside the truth of God, the values of the world are inverted, reminding us that God values those whom the world despises.

This is what Jesus was telling us as He knelt to wash the disciples' feet. He was saying, "This is obedience to God, not that you become great in the eyes of the world, but that you serve your neighbor." The style is clear—not only here, but throughout the gospel—the style is that of a servant.

It may be the same question, but we ask it to underscore the very heart of commitment—laying down our lives for the sake of Christ: Will you make My love your love? These questions beg for the focus of the issue in another question: If men cannot believe in Christians, whom they have seen, why should they believe in Christ, whom they have not seen?

They will never see Jesus unless they see Him in us—unless they see Him in the way we live.

Most Protestant churches removed from some of the early versions of the Apostle's Creed, "He descended into Hell." That's okay because there is scant biblical evidence for it; therefore, we don't need to make it a part of our basic creedal statement. But we need to recognize that it is experientially true. Jesus is with us in our hells. He has been there and He expressed it painfully on the cross, "My God, my God, why have you forsaken me?" (Matt. 27:46; Mark 15:34). He knows what it means to be human, to be in the hellish cauldron of our lives. In the same fashion, we need to be there for others in the hell of their lives, loving them for Christ. He continually asks the question: Will you love as I love?

Reflecting and Recording

Enabling us to respond to Jesus' challenge, "Will you really lay down your life for Me?" are these three questions: Will you make My will your will? Will you make My style your style? Will you love as I love?

With those four questions prompting you, write your prayer of commitment that you are going to follow Jesus.

Lord, thanks you for all you have given me. I ask for the strength and courage to live and love more like you in ways that others will see

During the Day *not me, but you in me.*

Copy your prayer on a card and keep it with you during the day, or put it in a place where you will see it often to repeat in prayer.

GROUP MEETING FOR WEEK TWO

• INTRODUCTION •

On Day Four of Week One, we considered our relationship to God in terms of contract or covenant, concluding that our relationship with God is a *covenant* one. We can look at the group relationship in the same way. There is a sense in which we have made a contract to be a part of this group and we want to honor that. But we want this to be a covenant relationship.

Much of our growth hinges upon our group participation. So, we want to be patient with one another, and share as openly and honestly as we can. Listen attentively to what people are saying; sometimes there is meaning beyond the surface of their words, which you may pick up if you are attentive.

Being a sensitive participant in this fashion is crucial. Responding immediately to the feeling we pick up is also crucial. Sometimes it is important for the group to focus its entire attention upon a particular individual. If some need or concern is expressed, it may be appropriate for the leader to ask the group to enter into a brief period of special prayer for the persons or concerns revealed. Participants should not always depend upon the leader for this kind of sensitivity, for the leader may miss it. Even if you aren't the leader, don't hesitate to ask the group to join you in a special prayer. This prayer may be silent, or someone may wish to lead aloud.

Remember, *everybody is a teacher and everybody is being taught.*

We each have a contribution to make to the group. What one considers trivial or unimportant may be just what another person needs to hear. We are not seeking to be profound, but simply to share our experience.

• SHARING TOGETHER •

Open the time together with the leader offering a brief prayer of thanksgiving for the opportunity of sharing with the group, and petitions for openness in sharing and loving response to each other.

1. Invite each person to share either the most meaningful or the most difficult day this week.

2. Invite two or three participants to describe one of the people they named on Days One and Two of this week who demonstrated a servant lifestyle.

3. Spend five to ten minutes discussing the difference between self-denial and self-depreciation.

4. Turn to your Reflecting and Recording on Day Three of this week. Spend some time discussing (each in turn) how God can use you as a servant to love the world, give grace and hope to the world, and bring light to dark places and beauty to ugliness.

5. On Day Four, we considered *the church as servant* as we reflected on Jesus' parable about the kingdom of heaven compared to a wedding feast, to which his servants had to go out and invite outcasts to come. You were asked to reflect on what particular groups in your community would be unlikely to come to the party, and whether your church would invite them to come. Spend ten to fifteen minutes discussing who the people are in your community that are not being reached, and whether your church could reach them if the church was willing to try.

6. On Day Five, we made the claim that outright betrayal is probably not a part of our experience, but denial might be. Spend ten to fifteen minutes discussing this. Be as honest and specific in confessing denial as you can be.

7. Leaders, when you have finished this discussion, invite the group to pray aloud together Psalm 51:1–4.

8. Invite two or three people to read aloud the way they wrote the last paragraph of Day Six in their time of Reflecting and Recording.

9. Spend the rest of the time discussing what it means for us to love as Jesus loved.

• PRAYING TOGETHER •

The effectiveness of this group and the quality of your covenant relationship will be enhanced by a commitment to pray for each other each day. Praying corporately each week in your meeting is a special ministry.

1. Take some time now for a period of verbal prayer. Invite people to make requests for special needs, situations, or relationships. When the sharing is complete, invite two or three persons to offer brief verbal prayers in response to these needs.
2. Tell the group to remember these needs as they pray for each other during the coming week. Close with the group praying together the Lord's Prayer, reminding them that you are linking yourselves with Christians of all time in universal praise, confession, thanksgiving, and intercession.

WEEK THREE

Promises, Promises

What's New about a "New Commandment"?

"A new command I give you: Love one another. As I have loved you, so you must love one another. By this everyone will know that you are my disciples, if you love one another."

—John 13:34–35

L ove your neighbor as yourself" was a commonplace principle among the Jewish people. It had a regular place in rabbinical teaching. In the various laws recorded in Leviticus 19, one is expressed this way: "Do not seek revenge or bear a grudge against anyone among your people, but love your neighbor as yourself. I am the LORD" (v. 18). Jesus was tested by an expert of the law, asking:

"Teacher, which is the greatest commandment in the Law?"

Jesus replied, "'Love the Lord your God with all your heart and with all your soul and with all your mind.' This is the first and greatest commandment. And the second is like it: 'Love your neighbor as yourself.' All the Law and the Prophets hang on these two commandments." (Matt. 22:36–40)

Even though He had underscored this familiar call to "love your neighbor as yourself," Jesus was obviously moving beyond what had been understood. A *new* commandment, He said. So what's new about this "new" commandment? The setting for Jesus' words provides at least a partial answer. They were celebrating Passover, and it was a family gathering. That these men were His family was evident in His address, "My children" (John 13:33).

He was tenderly preparing them for His death. He was going to leave them, and though they could not journey with Him, the door was open for them to follow, and be with Him again. The new commandment was not optional. It was in keeping this commandment that the Spirit of Jesus would flood through them and draw them together in a vibrant, living community stronger than life or death.

The new commandment was new because it was not law, but grace. It was based on a new covenant, which was being established, a new Passover to be sealed by Jesus' own blood. A new measure of love is set forth. The old command, "love your neighbor as yourself" (Lev. 19:18), was based on Mosaic law; Jesus was freely sharing love as a gift. So this love is grace, freely given, and it provides a new motive for relationship. As we are filled with the presence of Jesus Christ, the expression of His life becomes natural for us. With every other Christian, in the depth of our being, we feel like a brother or a sister because we are empowered by love that keeps loving through us.

Sometimes we are privileged to see it vividly and transparently. I once heard a sermon preached by E. V. Hill, a dynamic African American pastor serving in the Watts area of Los Angeles. He told this anecdote. The Watts riots were early signals of the explosive level to which race relations had gone in the 1960s. When the riots broke out in his neighborhood, he showed his courage, from his pulpit, denouncing those who were burning and destroying property, stealing from the merchants, and fostering fear throughout the community.

His preaching provoked all kinds of threats. Late one night, the phone rang. There was something about the way he held the receiver that told his wife something was wrong. When he hung up, she wanted to know who called and what they wanted. He didn't want to talk. She persisted, so he finally said, "I don't know who it was, but they've threatened to blow up my car with me in it."

Throughout the night, Hill was restless and uneasy. He couldn't sleep, worrying about the threat. About 2:00 a.m., he finally fell asleep. He awoke at 7:00 a.m., terrified. He reached over to touch his wife and she was not in bed. He couldn't find her anywhere in the house. He looked out the window, thinking she might have gone out on the patio. To his horror, she was not there. He then realized the car was gone from the carport. He was beside himself, about to call the police, when he saw her turn into the driveway and park the car.

He almost shouted, "Where have you been?"

Very calmly, she said, "I just wanted to drive the car around the block to make sure it was safe for you this morning."

"From that day on," Dr. Hill said, "I have never asked my wife if she loved me."

A hint, but a powerful one, of the new kind of love Jesus expressed on the cross, the love we are commanded to live.

Reflecting and Recording

Spend a few minutes in reflective response to the following questions:

What is the most vivid expression of love you have experienced in the past few months?

The way my husband cared for me during my long (3 month) convalescence from a fractured leg, waiting on me hand and foot, doing household chores including some he despised, while I could not.

How do you see love operating in the fellowship of your faith community?

The way they reach out to meet so many needs around us and out in the world, going themselves and sharing with faith partners, to see the work done.

During the Day

Move through the day, seeking to stay aware of opportunities of expressing a new kind of love.

A Place, Now and Then

Let not your heart be troubled: ye believe in God, believe also in me. In my Father's house are many mansions: if *it were* not *so*, I would have told you. I go to prepare a place for you. And if I go and prepare a place for you, I will come again, and receive you unto myself; that where I am, *there* ye may be also.

—John 14:1–3 KJV, emphasis added

In the summer of 1988, I preached at Marble Collegiate Church in New York, the church where Norman Vincent Peale became famous, and served for nearly forty years. After the worship, a small company of us had a baptismal service in Poling Chapel. I baptized a baby, Cordelia Clegg Istel, the granddaughter of one of my three dearest friends, Buford Dickinson. Buford was as close to me as a brother. We were college friends and seminary roommates. I was the best man in his wedding, and he in mine. He baptized one of my children, and all of our children grew up together.

Four years preceding this sacred event, he was smitten with cancer, and died after only a few months. That was as great a loss for me as the accidental death of my brother when he was in his mid-forties.

It was a memorable time—baptizing the grandbaby that Buford had never seen. In fact, I had performed the wedding ceremony of his daughter, Kathy, mother of Cordelia, after Buford's death.

As I held little Cordelia in my arms, and placed my watery hand on her head in baptism, I knew that Buford was rejoicing with us. As had been the case at Kathy's wedding, so now in this special service of baptism, I could feel Buford's presence—so could others in the group.

As I have noted, the baptismal service was held in Poling Chapel, a chapel named after Dan Poling, longtime minister of Marble Collegiate Church. Dr. Poling was a man of great faith and a powerful communicator. I remembered a story out of Dr. Poling's life. In 1921, he set out with his wife and children to go from New Hampshire to New York City in what was called a "touring car." As they were driving, something happened to the steering apparatus. The car went over an embankment, struck a telephone pole, and overturned.

Mrs. Poling and the children were injured, though not too seriously. Within a few minutes she managed to make her way to her husband who was pinned beneath the car. In desperation, Mrs. Poling kept calling his name, "Dan, Dan, Dan," over and over.

After a while, the ambulance came and took him to the hospital, where he fought for his life. After he had recuperated somewhat, he was trying to tell people what he remembered. "When I was down there, I kept hearing my wife's voice and knew the importance of listening to it, even though I wanted to slip away into the comfort of another world." The doctor interrupted and said, "Dr. Poling, had you ever stopped listening to your wife's voice, you would have died."

We Christians have a voice, a Presence, more vital and alive than Dr. Poling's wife or my friend Buford, a Presence that promises us His presence.

Here are some of the most revered words in Scripture. I deliberately use the King James Version because many have memorized this word of promise from that version. "Let not your heart be troubled . . ." (John 14:1). Many readers will quote the rest. We have heard it at countless funerals; simple words because that's the kind of words we need for consolation. As Alexander Maclaren said, "Simple words are the best clothing for the largest truths."[1]

A focal point in these chapters of John is the Greek word *mone,* which is translated "dwelling place," or a "place for you." We will consider this more as we journey on, but here, eleven disciples (Judas is no longer with them) are crushed at the thought of Jesus going away. What would they do if they lost Him?

What a puzzling word. "I'm going away, but I'm not going to leave you. You can abide in My presence, in joy, anticipating that one day you will join Me in the place I go to prepare for you" (author's paraphrase). There was no way for the disciples to understand these words. They had never heard anything like it.

As they listened during those hours, it became a bit clearer. Jesus was going to send the Paraclete, the Holy Spirit. We will consider this more on Day Seven of this week. For now, note that *Para* in Greek means "alongside," and the root of *kletos* is "to call." This Divine Companion Jesus promises to send will be alongside the disciples as Jesus has been.

In a real sense, though going away, Jesus would be *present* with them. His *Presence* would be "calling out" as encourager, counselor, helper, advocate, witness, and even as judge.

We know how difficult it is for us to stay in touch with, in *connection to* Christ through the Holy Spirit; how much more the disciples! Though they might believe He was going away, they did not know in what way that would happen, and they certainly knew nothing of the resurrection. Jesus was saying, "Trust Me."

Reflecting and Recording

Recall an occasion when you were called to trust. You didn't know what to do, you didn't understand what was being required or asked of you, the direction in which you were having to go was unclear, but you had to act, to move, to decide. Make some notes here about that experience to get it clearly in your mind.

Jim and I were married Feb. 6, 1964. Five days after the wedding he was required to leave for his new duty station at El Toro, CA, and planned to come back for me as soon as he had a place for us to settle. Two months later he was able to get leave and was not sure when he would be able to get it again, so I gave notice to my employer, packed up my things and our wedding gifts, and was ready to set out when he arrived. It was the first time I had ever left home and family to go and live in a place I did not know.

Was there anything in the experience you have recalled that enables you to better understand the deep trust that Jesus was calling from His disciples?

Half way through our journey, I found out that he did not have an apartment for us yet. I had been sending resumes to area newspapers about jobs but had no answers yet. All our worldly goods were in a 3×5 U-Haul trailer, with no home to take them to. I did pray and trust

During the Day

As you move through the day, look for the times, situations, and relationships when trust is required. *God to make it come out right, and yes, my prayer was answered. We found an apartment the day we arrived, and when I called my parents, a letter was waiting for me there asking me to call a newspaper in the area about a job, for which I interviewed and was hired.*

In My Father's House . . . Heaven

Let not your heart be troubled: ye believe in God, believe also in me. In my Father's house are many mansions: if *it were* not *so*, I would have told you. I go to prepare a place for you. And if I go and prepare a place for you, I will come again, and receive you unto myself; that where I am, *there* ye may be also.

—John 14:1–3 KJV, emphasis added

A re you listening? This is not a pep talk. Jesus was on His way to the cross. More than "brace yourself . . . chin up . . . we can win" was called for here. Jesus was leaving them, and He didn't have a lot of time to tell them what they need to know. They had been involved in a complex conversation. When Jesus announced He was leaving them, the disciples responded as you and I would—Where? Why? When? Can we go? Eventuating in Peter making his rash statement, "Why can't I follow you now? I will lay down my life for you" (John 13:37).

Jesus moved to talk as simply and as clearly as He could. "Come on, guys, center down, listen to what I'm saying. You believe in God, so believe in Me. God is our Father, and in His house there are many rooms. I'm going to be with the Father, and I'm going to get a place ready for you, because someday I'm coming back, and I will take you with Me to the Father's house, where we will be together always" (author's paraphrase).

What magnificent simplicity! Mourning hearts, through the ages, have found hope and peace in this straightforward word of their Savior. The image may have been more immediately clear to the disciples than to us. It was a practice in that day, given the nature of travel, for someone in a traveling party to go ahead of the group and make arrangements for lodging and food. In fact, they were meeting that night when Jesus spoke these words in a room that had been prepared for them ahead of time. So His word was understood: "I go to prepare a place for you" (John 14:2 KJV).

That place? "In my Father's house are many mansions" (v. 2). Jesus was talking about heaven, the eternal abode of Father, Son, and Holy Spirit; the future abode of those who have accepted Jesus' promise of eternal life with Him.

A spate of books and movies about heaven have been released in recent years, responding to our boundless curiosity. But our curiosity will never be completely satisfied until the experience is personally ours. Jesus addressed that curiosity and our doubts as well: "Let not your heart be troubled: ye believe in God, believe also in me. In my Father's house are many mansions: if it were not so, I would have told you" (vv. 1–2). He was saying right off, "Trust Me. This is big and awesome, a lot of mystery surrounds it, but I'm telling you how it is, and how it is going to be" (author's paraphrase).

Not an expansive description of heaven, but enough in this brief word to give us all we need, not to satisfy our curiosity, but to whet our longing as we anticipate eternal life with Jesus. Though everything in Scripture supports the fact that heaven is a *state,* a relationship, a condition, it also is a *place,* a place in the great universe of God. Think about it. In His resurrection, Jesus has a glorified body. That body is *somewhere*, and as He promises, where He is, there His servants will also be.

In that place, there is ample room. One of my favorite spirituals is titled "Plenty Good Room."

Plenty good room, plenty good room,
Plenty good room in my Father's kingdom
Plenty good room, plenty good room,
So choose your seat and sit down.

As simple as it sounds, it has profound meaning. It is a theological statement about the inclusiveness of God, the God who has many dwelling places. Think of it personally. Despite our imperfections, God chooses you and me. Despite our failures, God chooses you and me. Despite your past, despite my past, God chooses us. Despite our sinful present, God chooses us by making it clear that there is plenty good room. Despite our shortcomings, God makes room for us.

Now think more deeply in terms of how we differ from Jesus. He has the capacity to embrace those who have been rejected. His ministry gives comfort to those whom we might think should be excluded. Be honest: if we were making the decision about who has room in the Father's kingdom, we would most likely limit the number of those who could have a place. Some of us would only have a heaven that includes people just like us and excludes those who are not like us.

Jesus says that in the Father's house there are many mansions, or plenty good room.

One other word: our place (mansion) is *with God*. There is only one other occasion in Scripture, later in this same chapter of John's Gospel, in which the word translated "mansions" is used. "Anyone who loves me will obey my teaching. My Father will love them, and we will come to them and make our home [abode] with them" (v. 23). Our *home*, heaven, is in God. God's dwelling place is in us.

When I think of it this way, I think of the prodigal son, concentrating more on the loving father. For a long time, after each of our children left home, we kept their room just as it was when they left. I think that is the way it was with the father in the parable. Brokenhearted because of the son's leaving, the father kept hope and he demonstrated that hope by keeping the son's room as it was when he left. When the son returned, he accepted him as though he had never been away. Our heavenly Father is keeping a room for us, ready for our occupancy.

Reflecting and Recording

Spend some time thinking about the meaning of the compassion of Jesus for us—His inclusive invitation and promise.

To have compassion toward someone else, we must understand Christ's compassion for us. Ask yourself: *Does the way I live and the way I relate to others reflect my awareness of Christ's compassion for me?*

If we are willing, and if we reflected Christ's compassion for us, we could reach out to the unlovable and show them love! Doesn't that mean that if we are willing, we can embrace the shunned and show him or her acceptance?

If we are willing, we can embrace the sinner and he or she can experience the love of God.

Be specific now in your thinking. Do you know anyone or any group that is shunned? Or, even if you don't name them as such, you see them as sinners? Name the person or group here.

If so, are you willing, and how will you show acceptance and love? Make some notes here.

During the Day

Look diligently for someone or some situation in which you can express the compassion of Christ.

The Promise of Presence

"Do not let your hearts be troubled. You believe in God; believe also in me. My Father's house has many rooms; if that were not so, would I have told you that I am going there to prepare a place for you? And if I go and prepare a place for you, I will come back and take you to be with me that you also may be where I am. You know the way to the place where I am going."

Thomas said to him, "Lord, we don't know where you are going, so how can we know the way?"

Jesus answered, "I am the way and the truth and the life. No one comes to the Father except through me. If you really know me, you will know my Father as well. From now on, you do know him and have seen him."

—John 14:1–7

Don't forget the setting. Jesus was having His last meal with His disciples. This was His final quality time with them. His words were not public proclamation, but the intimate sharing with a few faithful friends. Imagine yourself there, listening.

This was the day before His crucifixion; Jesus was getting ready to leave them. They couldn't comprehend what this leaving really meant. He assured them that there would always be a path for them to take to follow and find Him.

Why does Jesus have to go somewhere without them? How long will He be gone? Why can't they go with Him? Questions, questions, questions. But such questions would someday be answered. In the midst of that intense conversation, Judas (not the betrayer), a lesser-known disciple, asked a question that focuses the issue even more sharply, making it probingly personal, "Lord, how is it that you will manifest yourself to us . . . ?" (v. 22 RSV). The question might be: How are You going to be real to us?

In this fourteenth chapter of John, Jesus makes some almost unbelievable promises. First, there is the promise of presence. Jesus gave them that hopeful benediction in verses 1 and 2: "Let not your hearts be troubled; believe in God, believe also in Me. In My Father's house are many rooms; if it were not so, would I have told you that I go and prepare a place for you?" (author's paraphrase). Thomas pressed Jesus about what He meant, assuring Jesus that they neither knew where He was going, nor did they know the way.

Again, it wasn't easy for them to understand, because Jesus said, "I am the way" (v. 6). Then came the most dramatic word. Jesus explained to them that to know Him was to know the Father. Again Philip pressed the issue, expressing the deep human longing: "Lord, show us the Father, and we shall be satisfied" (v. 8 RSV).

Jesus made the point as emphatically as possible; indeed, there's even a hint of impatience in Jesus' answer: "Have I been with you so long, and yet you do not know me, Philip? He who has seen me has seen the Father; how can you say, 'Show us the Father'? Do you not believe that I am in the Father and the Father in me?" (John 14:9–10 RSV).

Arthur John Gossip, the great Scottish preacher, called that paragraph the most staggering saying to be found in human literature. Think about it. There Philip and the others were, sitting with Jesus, this man like them, with hands rough from his work as a carpenter, speaking as though who He really was should be self-evident. He was shocked that Philip would think He had to prove Himself other than He had already done. But we can identify with Philip. He and his friends had walked and talked and eaten with Jesus. He was one "like them." Philip was obviously shocked that Jesus was shocked. We, too, would have been stunned by Jesus' challenge: "How can you say, 'Show us the Father?' If you have seen Me, you have seen the Father" (author's paraphrase).

Follow Philip to calvary. Don't you imagine his request, "Show us the Father," was tumbling around more boisterously as he saw Jesus humiliated and strung up on the cross as a criminal? In overwhelming frustration, might he have been thinking, *That . . . that is the Father?*

But Jesus went even beyond this claim of showing the Father and this promise of going to prepare a place; He promised His presence to lead us there: "I will not leave you desolate; I will come to you. Yet a little while, and the world will see me no more, but you will see me; because I live, you will live also" (vv. 18–19 RSV). We will focus on this promise tomorrow.

Richard Baxter was an Anglican priest in seventeenth-century London. Both he and his wife suffered a lot of illnesses, which led to his writing the hymn "Lord, It Belongs Not to My Care."

Lord, it belongs not to my care
Whether I die or live;
To love and serve Thee is my share,
And this Thy grace must give.

If life be long, I will be glad,
That I may long obey;
If short, yet why should I be sad
To welcome endless day?

Christ leads me through no darker rooms
Than He went through before;
He that unto God's kingdom comes
Must enter by this door.

Come, Lord, when grace hath made me meet
Thy blessed face to see;
For if Thy work on earth be sweet
What will Thy glory be!

Then I shall end my sad complaints
And weary sinful days,
And join with the triumphant saints
That sing my Savior's praise.

My knowledge of that life is small,

The eye of faith is dim;

But 'tis enough that He knows all,

And I shall be with Him.

Reflecting and Recording

Read the hymn again, slowly and reflectively.

Now concentrate on the last stanza. In a few sentences, restate that stanza in your own words.

I don't, and can't, really know what heaven will be like. I don't always understand the things that happen in this life. But I do know that Jesus knows and understands everything, including me, so I don't have to worry about it. When I am with Him for eternity, I will either know and understand, or no longer need to, because He does and I am with Him.

During the Day

Find occasions throughout the day to affirm to yourself, *Christ knows all and I will be with Him.*

The Way, the Truth, the Life

Thomas said to him, "Lord, we don't know where you are going, so how can we know the way?"

Jesus answered, "I am the way and the truth and the life. No one comes to the Father except through me. If you really know me, you will know my Father as well. From now on, you do know him and have seen him."

—John 14:5–7

Jesus wants us to know who He is. Seemingly, His favorite way of doing that is captured in what we call His "I am" sayings. I am the Bread of Life. I am the Good Shepherd. I am the Door. I am the True Vine. I am the Resurrection and the Life. I am the Alpha and the Omega.

These descriptive identities were from the common life of the people, and He used them in the particular setting in which He was, and in connection with what was going on in His relationships and conversations. His claim, "I am the bread of life," illustrates this. He had fed the five thousand (see John 6), and left the crowd, crossing the lake to Capernaum. They followed there, wanting to know why He had left them.

Jesus answered, "Very truly I tell you, you are looking for me, not because you saw the signs I performed but because you ate the loaves and had your fill. Do not work for food that spoils, but for food that endures to eternal life, which the Son of Man will give you. For on him God the Father has placed his seal of approval."

Then they asked him, "What must we do to do the works God requires?"

Jesus answered, "The work of God is this: to believe in the one he has sent."

So they asked him, "What sign then will you give that we may see it and believe you? What will you do? Our ancestors ate the manna in the wilderness; as it is written: 'He gave them bread from heaven to eat.'"

Jesus said to them, "Very truly I tell you, it is not Moses who has given you the bread from heaven, but it is my Father who gives you the true bread from heaven. For the bread of God is the bread that comes down from heaven and gives life to the world."

"Sir," they said, "always give us this bread."

Then Jesus declared, "I am the bread of life. Whoever comes to me will never go hungry, and whoever believes in me will never be thirsty." (John 6:26–35)

In His great "I am" claims, Jesus tells us who He is and who God is. He invites us to come into His presence, listen to Him, receive His love, accept His forgiveness, and live in Him.

In this intimate gathering with His disciples in the upper room, He made His most comprehensive "I am" claim: "I am the way and the truth and the life" (John 14:6). He is the *way* because in Him the *truth* of the Father is revealed. That truth is not in concepts or ideals, but through coming to know Him, and we know Him through Jesus, so Jesus is *life*.

It is important to keep in mind what Jesus is responding to. He was seeking to prepare His disciples for His coming death, and began by making the promise of going away to prepare a place for them. He made the statement, "You know the way to the place I am going." This was shocking and confusing, and Thomas said to Him, "Lord, we don't know where you are going, so how can we know the way?" (see John 14:1–5).

Jesus was saying, "You do know the way, because *I am the way*, and I am the way because *I am the truth and the life*" (author's paraphrase). The second and third words—truth and life—are explanatory of the first; they show how the first is true. Jesus is *the way*; He is the truest and clearest representation of the divine nature we have ever had, or can ever have. This is what John was saying in his prologue to this Gospel: the Word became flesh; in Him was life, and that life was the light of men (see John 1:1, 4). This is what Paul was saying in his Epistles: He is "the image of the invisible God" (Col. 1:15) and He is "the image and glory of God" (1 Cor. 11:7).

What drama is in this setting, talking about *being life* when He was headed for His death! Thus the core truth of the gospel: the only way He is giving life is by giving up His physical life for us. His death is the gateway to life for us.

Reflecting and Recording

One of the meaningful spiritual disciplines of my life has been memorizing. I wish I had been introduced to this discipline early in my Christian walk, especially memorizing Scripture. This has also included memorizing stanzas of hymns. Yesterday, I introduced a hymn I discovered in the last few years. I invite you to join me in memorizing the last verse of that hymn.

> My knowledge of that life is small,
> The eye of faith is dim;
> But 'tis enough that He knows all,
> And I shall be with Him.

During the Day

If you have not memorized the words, copy them and take them with you during the day. Find occasions to quote them aloud, or register them in your memory, or read them, claiming Christ's presence now and in the future.

DAY SIX

The Glorious Partnership

"Very truly I tell you, whoever believes in me will do the works I have been doing, and they will do even greater things than these, because I am going to the Father. And I will do whatever you ask in my name, so that the Father may be glorified in the Son. You may ask me for anything in my name, and I will do it."

—JOHN 14:12–14

The Bible is full of promises, fantastic promises; many of them coming from Jesus himself: "Because I live, you also will live" (John 14:19). "I will never leave you nor forsake you" (Josh 1:5). "Come to me, all who labor and are heaven laden, and I will give you rest" (Matt. 11:28 RSV). "Abide in me, and I [will abide] in you" (John 15:4 KJV). "You shall receive power when the Holy Spirit has come upon you" (Acts 1:8 RSV). "I am with you always, to the very end of the age" (Matt. 28:20).

Fantastic promises, but none more fantastic than the two we have here in the text for today. The King James Bible and the Revised Standard Version respectively introduce these promises with Jesus saying, "Verily, verily, I say unto you," and "Truly, truly, I say to you," insisting that we stand our minds at attention and listen. We are about to hear something wonderful. The Jerusalem Bible begins, "I tell you most solemnly," and the New English Bible has it, "In truth, in very truth I tell you."

Jesus is saying, "Are you listening? I am about to disclose something that you can receive with unfaltering confidence. It is coming on My authority." And when He speaks, it takes our breath away. "Greater things than I have done will you do. Ask anything in My name and I will do it" (author's paraphrase).

In these two promises, Jesus invites us into a glorious partnership, a partnership of acting and praying.

I often begin my teaching on prayer by asking a probing question: What if there are some things God either cannot or will not do until, and unless, people pray? Scripture teaches clearly that God has chosen to order His kingdom economy by making prayer a part of the enterprise. It is clear, not only from Scripture but from our Christian history, that God's promises to act in our personal lives and in community are often connected with conditions we are to meet. One of those conditions often set down is prayer.

The classic example of this in the Old Testament is 2 Chronicles 7:14: "If my people, who are called by my name, will humble themselves and pray and seek my face and turn from their wicked ways . . ." Those are the conditions. And if we meet those conditions, God says, "then will I hear from heaven, and I will forgive their sin and will heal their land."

The classic example in the New Testament is John 15:7: "If you remain in me and my words remain in you . . ." Those are the conditions; if we meet them, then Jesus says, "ask whatever you wish, and it will be done for you."

The partnership involves our praying, but also our acting. But even that has conditions. "Anyone who has faith," Jesus says, "will do the things I have been doing" (author's paraphrase). What a glorious partnership: Christ doing for us, in response to our praying; the other, Christ working on us and in us so that our acting is His, and His acting is ours.

We will be reflecting more on this in the balance of our sitting with Christ in this intimate conversation, because He will talk more about He and the Father living in us and acting through us. Tomorrow we will reflect on the power that is ours as we make real this glorious partnership.

Earlier in chapter 6 of John's Gospel, the disciples asked Jesus, "'What must we do to do the works God requires?' Jesus answered, 'The work of God is this: to believe in the one he has sent'" (vv. 28–29).

Note that they asked about works; Jesus responded in the singular by talking about work. Think about this: our primary work, our work that defines everything else in the Christian faith, is "to believe in the one he has sent." Our relationship to God is the deepest thing about us. If that is right, all other things will be right; if that is wrong, nothing else can be as right as it might be.

We usually credit Paul with stating the doctrine of salvation in terms of justification by grace through faith. To be sure Paul, in his Epistles, developed that teaching in a systematic way. Yet, here Jesus has planted the seeds that produce the glorious fruit of Paul's teaching. Jesus' statement, "The work of God is this: to believe in the one he has sent," is the germ of everything Paul taught.

Reflecting and Recording

Spend a few minutes reflecting on the fact that Jesus' statement is the germ of everything Paul taught about the law being of no avail for our salvation. Faith alone has the unfailing power to bring us to eternal life.

During the Day

As you perform works today that may be considered your Christian work, reflect on how your doing that work is shaped by your believing in Christ.

The Gift of the Helper

"If you love me, keep my commands. And I will ask the Father, and he will give you another advocate to help you and be with you forever—the Spirit of truth. The world cannot accept him, because it neither sees him nor knows him. But you know him, for he lives with you and will be in you. I will not leave you as orphans; I will come to you. Before long, the world will not see me anymore, but you will see me. Because I live, you also will live. On that day you will realize that I am in my Father, and you are in me, and I am in you. Whoever has my commands and keeps them is the one who loves me. The one who loves me will be loved by my Father, and I too will love them and show myself to them."

Then Judas (not Judas Iscariot) said, "But, Lord, why do you intend to show yourself to us and not to the world?"

Jesus replied, "Anyone who loves me will obey my teaching. My Father will love them, and we will come to them and make our home with them. Anyone who does not love me will not obey my teaching. These words you hear are not my own; they belong to the Father who sent me.

"All this I have spoken while still with you. But the Advocate, the Holy Spirit, whom the Father will send in my name, will teach you all things and will remind you of everything I have said to you."

—JOHN 14:15–26

Verse 18, in the varying translations says, He will not leave us: *comfortless, desolate, alone,* or *bereft.* A number of translations say He will not leave us *as orphans.* It's a poignant rendering. Jesus is concerned about His little flock, so He assures them that He will send an "advocate" (v. 16). The Greek word is *Paraclete,* and its richness is missed in any single word such as "Helper," "Counselor," "Comforter," or "Advocate." Phillips translates verse 18 like this: "I am not going to leave you alone in the world—I am coming to you."

In the Greek *para* means "alongside" and the root of *kletos* is "to call." So this Divine Companion Jesus promises to send will be alongside the disciples as Jesus has been. What a promise, "calling out" as encourager, counselor, helper, advocate, witness, and even as judge. That's what Paraclete means.

The Paraclete, the Holy Spirit, our Divine Companion, is the promised gift of the Father sent at the Son's request. He is given only to those who have received and loved the Son. The Spirit is not given to the world, which neither sees nor knows Christ. He is given to those who have known and obey Christ.

Amazing, and not yet fully appropriated by most Christians. Jesus had been the Paraclete during His earthly life; now, He was going to provide someone to take His place. The Father will give "another advocate" who will abide with these disciples forever (v. 16).

Jesus said, "I will come to you" (v. 18). His resurrected life will be shared through the Paraclete. The Father will also come, for Jesus said later, "Anyone who loves me will obey my teaching. My Father will love them, and we will come to them and make our home with them" (v. 23). The Persons of the Godhead, the Trinity—Father, Son, and Holy Spirit—come as the Paraclete to abide, encourage, empower, and witness through the disciples. No wonder the disciples will never be orphans.

Jesus repeatedly emphasized that the Paraclete is the "Spirit of truth" (v. 17). He will enlighten and open up the words and works of Jesus. We easily forget how crucial this is. Imagine the feeling of lostness on the part of the disciples. They had listened as Jesus taught during His earthly ministry. They were mystified, and had certainly not grasped it all.

Jesus knew they were bewildered, so He was quick to assure them that all would be made plain to them when the "Teacher" came. Not only would He make plain, He would also bring to mind things Jesus had said which would otherwise be forgotten (v. 26).

There are always those who insist the Spirit takes us beyond Jesus to "newer and deeper truth." Not so. The Spirit is always under the authority of Jesus, clarifying, making clear

His teaching and ministry. We need to remember He comes in Jesus' name to unfold Jesus' meaning for all men. The Paraclete is subject to Jesus!

Reflecting and Recording

Look at the dynamic in which this promise of the Holy Spirit is set. The praying Christ and the giving Father: "I will ask and he will give." What does this say to you about Christ who ever "lives to make intercession for [us]" (Heb. 7:25 RSV)?

He is not only our way to heaven and our guide for life on earth. When we do not even have the words or the knowledge to ask for what we truly need, He asks for us, because He knows it all and loves us.

The abiding gift: Jesus will send another Counselor, who will abide with us forever. Rehearse a portion of what we asserted above: the Persons of the Godhead, the Trinity—Father, Son, and Holy Spirit—come as the Paraclete to abide, encourage, empower, and witness through the disciples.

During the Day

Be sensitive as you move through the day to those occasions when you need to intentionally invite the Paraclete to be with you: to help, to comfort, and to guide.

GROUP MEETING FOR WEEK THREE

• INTRODUCTION •

Two essential ingredients for a Christian fellowship are feedback and follow-up. Follow-up is essential to express Christian concern and ministry.

The leader is primarily responsible for feedback in the group, but all should be encouraged to share their feelings about how the group is functioning. Listening is essential. To listen to another, we are saying, "You are important; I value you." It is also crucial to check out meaning in order that those who are sharing this pilgrimage will know that we really hear them. We often mis-hear. "Are you saying [fill in the blank]?" is a good check question. It takes only a couple of people in the group who listen to give feedback in this fashion to set the mood for the group.

Follow-up is the function of everyone. If we listen to what others are saying, we will discover needs and concerns beneath the surface and situations that deserve special prayer and attention. Participants might want to take notes of these as the group shares. Follow up during the week with a telephone call, a written note of encouragement, and a visit.

• SHARING TOGETHER •

By this time, a significant amount of intimacy should exist in the group. Participants should at least beginning to feel safe, perhaps more willing to share. Still there is no place for pressure. The leader, however, should coax openness. Every person is a gift to the group. The gift is fully given by sharing.

1. Invite two or three persons to share the most vivid expression of love they have experienced in the past few months.

2. Leaders, ask the group to read aloud with you John 14:1–3 (Day Three). Invite two or three persons to share an experience when this text was deeply meaningful to them.

3. Spend 25–30 minutes discussing heaven. Talk about the way you understand heaven. Discuss the fact of Jesus' promise of "many rooms" is a statement about the inclusiveness of God . . . that heaven is the *presence of God,* but it is also a *place.* What beliefs about heaven have been challenged by what you have been studying this week? Were there any new ideas?

4. Invite someone to read Richard Baxter's hymn (on Day Four). Then invite two or three people to read how they rewrote the last stanza of that hymn in their Reflecting and Recording on Day Four.

5. Spend five minutes discussing the last two lines of the hymn: "But 'tis enough that He knows all, And I shall be with Him." Is that belief enough?

6. Spend ten minutes discussing the claims: (1) that God's promises to act in our personal lives and in history are connected with conditions we are to meet, and (2) to be effective, our action must be accompanied by faith.

7. Spend the rest of your time discussing the praying Christ and the giving Father: "I will ask and he will give." What does this say to about Christ who ever "lives to make intercession for [us]" (Heb. 7:25 RSV)?

• PRAYING TOGETHER •

Most of us are not comfortable with long periods of silent prayer when we are in a group. At the same time, many of us are not comfortable praying aloud. We should acknowledge the fact that silent thoughts and prayers are as important as verbal prayers. We need to practice both.

1. Spend five minutes, first, in silent prayer in this fashion. (Leaders should keep the time.) Pray specifically for two people. Look around the group and select those you are going to pray for in this time of prayer. Silently, deliberately bring one of the persons you have chosen with you into the presence of the Father in this fashion: imagine that you are introducing that person to the Father. Think about what you know about that person.

Tell the Father those things and ask Him to be present with him/her and to bless him/her in ways that will be responsive to what you have shared about the person. (The leader will announce when two minutes have passed and you will begin to close your prayer for the first person, and repeat the exercise with the second person you selected.)

2. Pray corporately, silently, and aloud. Invite each person in the group to share a special need, concern, or joy. After each person shares, invite the group to offer prayers for the person, either silently or a brief two- or three-sentence verbal prayer.

3. Close your prayer time with the group praying together:

Heavenly Father, you have promised to hear what we ask in the Name of your Son: Accept and fulfill our petitions, we pray, not as we ask in our ignorance, nor as we deserve in our sinfulness, but as you know and love us in your Son Jesus Christ our Lord. Amen.[1]

Christ's Chosen People

Greater Things Than I Have Done

"Very truly I tell you, whoever believes in me will do the works I have been doing, and they will do even greater things than these, because I am going to the Father. And I will do whatever you ask in my name, so that the Father may be glorified in the Son. You may ask me for anything in my name, and I will do it."

—John 14:12–14

The pages of the Old and the New Testament are punctuated with promises—all sorts of promises of God's offer of life and meaning to us. Here is one of the most breathtaking: "Very truly I tell you, whoever believes in me will do the works I have been doing, and they will do even greater things than these, because I am going to the Father" (John 14:12).

If this is even remotely possible, then mustn't we confess we have never taken Jesus seriously? The least we have to confess is that we have certainly been satisfied with far less than He has in mind for us as His followers.

Are you listening? The promise is for us to claim.

Charles Schultz, the artist who created the *Peanuts* cartoons, is one of my favorite theologians. In one series, he has Snoopy, that hound of heaven, saying of Woodstock, that would-be bird of paradise: "Someday, Woodstock is going to be a great eagle." Then in the next frame he says, "He is going to soar thousands of feet above the ground." Woodstock takes off into the air, and as Snoopy looks on, he sees the bird upside-down, whirling around crazily. So he has second thoughts. In the third frame Snoopy says, "Well, maybe hundreds of feet above the ground . . ." But hardly had the words gotten out of his mouth, when

Woodstock plummets to the ground and lies there, on his back dazed, and Snoopy has to conclude, "Maybe he will be one of those eagles who just walks around."

Isn't it amazing how quickly we settle for less than is promised, and for far less than is possible?

So what have we here in this word of Jesus? The dramatic power of it becomes more pronounced as we keep in mind who said it. Jesus said it—the Man who came to save the world. The Man who forgave and loved, and washed His disciples' feet. The Man who made the lame to walk and the blind to see. The Man who calmed the storm and took little children on His lap and blessed them. The Man who ate with sinners and flung His life into the teeth of the raw and rampant prejudice of His day by conversing with the Samaritan woman at the well. The Man who finished all the work God gave Him to do—and is now seated at the right hand of the Father, crowned with glory and honor. Can you believe it? That's the Man who says to you and me, "Very truly I tell you, whoever believes in me will do the works I have been doing, and they will do even greater things than these, because I am going to the Father" (John 14:12).

Do you believe it? Do you believe it enough to start the process in your mind of claiming the promise? Stop reading for a few minutes and ponder the promise.

Our problem is that we trust in Jesus with some things, some of the time, when we need to trust Him with all things all of the time.

Do you think Jesus might be saying, "You are more than you think you are"? It is so easy to sink into feelings of weakness and inadequacy, and begin to ensnare ourselves in self-depreciation, and think far less of ourselves than we ought to think. It happens to most of us. It happens to me.

When I am feeling down on myself, when depression threatens to turn the sky of my life into dark clouds of gloom, when I sense I am becoming preoccupied with failure, I try to remember the eighth psalm. A portion of it goes:

When I consider your heavens, the work of your fingers, the moon and the stars, which you have set in place, what is mankind that you are mindful of them, human beings that you care for them?

You have made them a little lower than the angels and crowned them with glory and honor. (vv. 3–5)

Do you remember it? The English Revised Version has it "but a little lower than God, and crownest him with glory and honour."

If I can put this word of the psalmist together with what Jesus said, then I can know that I am more than I think I am.

But you press the question. How can I believe that I am more than I think I am? Listen! You are important to God. In fact you are a unique, unrepeatable miracle of God. You have that on the authority of God's Word. Don't you remember? Jesus said it, not a sparrow falls to the earth without the will of the Father . . . and you are worth more value than many sparrows (see Matthew 10:29, 31). He stated it even more graphically when He said, "even the very hairs of your head are all numbered" (Matt. 10:30). That is the witness of Scripture. You are important to God.

That means there is a place in God's heart that only you can fill. That's the message of the Book. God loves each one of us as though each one of us were the only person in the world to love. If you were the only person in the world, God would have still sent His Son to save you.

Reflecting and Recording

Write a few sentences expressing your thoughts and feelings in response to the following statements:

You are more than you think you are.

I ask for strength and faith to live up to God's promise for me. Let me embrace all that he meant me to be, and seek his guidance to be that person.

There is a place in God's heart that only you can fill.

This makes me ever more grateful for God's love, grace and mercy, and for the ongoing care and blessings I receive.

On Day Five of last week I talked about memorization as a spiritual discipline, and invited you to memorize a stanza of a hymn. I memorized this promise of Jesus years ago, and it has been a mainstay in my arsenal of spiritual strength and hope. Seek to memorize it now, or copy it so you can carry it with you.

"Very truly I tell you, whoever believes in me will do the works I have been doing, and they will do even greater things than these, because I am going to the Father." (John 14:12)

During the Day

Whenever a difficult situation or relationship arises today, quote this promise of Jesus and remember that you are more than you think you are.

Whatever You Ask in My Name

"Very truly I tell you, whoever believes in me will do the works I have been doing, and they will do even greater things than these, because I am going to the Father. And I will do whatever you ask in my name, so that the Father may be glorified in the Son. You may ask me for anything in my name, and I will do it."

—John 14:12–14

When Jesus begins with the words, "Verily, verily!" (KJV), He is bidding us to listen with our utmost attention. We understand that, having considered yesterday the first fantastic promise that followed His mind-grabbing, "Very truly I tell you" was "greater things than I have done will you do" (John 14:12, author's paraphrase).

The point was made that Jesus might be saying, "You are more than you think you are." It was suggested that our problem is that we trust Jesus with some things, some of the time, when we need to trust Him with all things all of the time.

As if one fantastic promise is not enough to make us breathless, Jesus gives that equally fantastic promise, "I will do whatever you ask in my name, so that the Father may be glorified in the Son" (v. 13).

These two promises are intimately connected, solidly bound. "Whoever believes in me will do the works I have been doing" . . . and the ground for that? "Because I am going to the Father" (v. 12). He continued, "And whatever you ask, if you believe, I will do" (v. 13, author's paraphrase). This is a hint of what Jesus will make clearer in His metaphor of the vine and the branches.

I am the vine, ye are the branches: He that abideth in me, and I in him, the same bringeth forth much fruit: for without me ye can do nothing. . . . If ye abide in me, and my words abide in you, ye shall ask what ye will, and it shall be done unto you. Herein is my Father glorified, that ye bear much fruit; so shall ye be my disciples. (John 15:5, 7–8 KJV).

Our praying and our acting are connected and both are dependent upon our believing and sharing the life of Christ.

It is worth noting that John did not record the ascension of our Lord. Yet, the meaning of the ascension is fully expressed. Ponder the way Mark told the story: "After the Lord Jesus had spoken to them, he was taken up into heaven and he sat at the right hand of God. Then the disciples went out and preached everywhere, and the Lord worked with them and confirmed his word by the signs that accompanied it" (Mark 16:19–20).

See how expansive Jesus' presence is. He is seated at the right hand of God, but He is working with His followers to confirm that His work goes on. That's the connection between the two fantastic promises He made: "Greater works" and "Ask and I will do it." Are you listening? Jesus takes two paths for His kingdom to come. One, doing for us in response to our prayers. Two, working on us and in us so that our acts are His and His acts are ours.

It is instructive to note that Jesus linked His amazing promise that we would do greater works than He had done with His equally amazing promise about prayer: "I will do whatever you ask in my name, so that the Father may be glorified in the Son. You may ask me for anything in my name, and I will do it" (vv. 13–14).

Do you notice that He said the same thing twice? It is obvious that He wanted that to register in our minds. So get the full impact of what Jesus wanted to convey. Pay close attention to the verb tense. Jesus did not say, "Ask anything in My name and I might do it." He didn't say, "Ask, and there is a good chance that what you ask for you will get." No, He was very emphatic: "Ask me for anything in my name, and I will do it" (v. 14).

It may seem extravagant and extreme, but look closely. We need to register the fact that the promise Jesus gives us here is not unconditional. Rather, this promise is explicitly and strictly limited. It is only what we ask for in Christ's name, only what we pray for His sake, that He promises to give us.

So we can confidently count on receiving what we ask for, only if what we ask will advance God's cause and bring God glory.

I am convinced that the primary reason most of us are not empowered to live more effective Christian lives is that we don't spend enough time on our knees. As asserted earlier, we trust Jesus with some things some of the time, when we need to trust Him with all things all of the time. We don't believe what Jesus said.

Our praying and our acting are connected, and both are dependent upon our believing and sharing the life of Christ.

Reflecting and Recording

Spend a few minutes answering this question in your mind: When was the last time I attempted something so great for God that I knew I would fail unless I was empowered by Christ though the Holy Spirit?

Far, for too long ago, in a conversation with my then-13-year-old son, who is now 49. The conversation did not have the desired result immediately, but thanks be to God, appears to have planted a seed that bloomed in later years.

During the Day

Look for someone today, perhaps call a person you may be sharing this study journey with, and discuss these two radical promises: "Greater things than I have done will you do," and "Ask anything in my name and I will do it."

Peace

"All this I have spoken while still with you. But the Advocate, the Holy Spirit, whom the Father will send in my name, will teach you all things and will remind you of everything I have said to you. Peace I leave with you; my peace I give you. I do not give to you as the world gives. Do not let your hearts be troubled and do not be afraid."

—John 14:25–27

This is one of the most power-packed and comforting passages in the Gospels. The promise of the Holy Spirit and its fulfillment hovers over everything that follows. We will be contemplating this promise on a number of days next week. For now, let's deal with the gift Jesus offers: peace.

As you read the passage, did you note this defining phrase, "not give to you as the world gives"? In a negative way, it tells us what kind of peace Christ gives. The world defines peace through rule of law. There is ongoing discussion in society about how to keep the peace. We not only talk about peace in that way when we think of international conflict, we talk about it in our cities where racial strife flares into open conflict and even killing. We abhor civic violence and war involving our nation. The kind of peace that the world gives is through law and order kept by the aggressive use of force.

And then there is personal peace that the world offers. The late advice columnist Ann Landers received something like ten thousand letters a month. When asked what the most common subject people wanted help with, she said it was *fear*. Most people seem to be afraid of something; afraid of losing their health, their job, or their family; afraid of upsetting their neighbor or alienating a friend. So the peace the world offers are ways to evade or resolve conflict, to conquer or live with fear.

Political and personal peace for these issues is possible, and we can achieve it, but it is short-lived if it comes from human effort.

It is not the kind of peace Jesus gives, and it's not the way His peace comes. Jesus' peace is a gift and it comes through surrender. If we obey His Word, He and the Father will make their home in us, in our hearts, abiding there to bring peace, not by force but by choice.

The peace Christ gives is primarily the peace of His presence. This is the source for the peace of forgiveness. Even the peace of a clear conscience comes from our relationship with Christ and keeping our spiritual house in order.

Though the United States didn't enter into World War II until December 1941, war had begun in Europe much earlier. In 1934, Adolf Hitler summoned many of the leaders of the German church to his Berlin office and berated them for insufficiently supporting his programs. From that point on, there was a struggle between the church and Hitler's government. Pastor Martin Niemöller was one of the people who stood strong in opposition. Early in the struggle there was a confrontation between Hitler and Pastor Niemöller. Hitler snapped, "You confine yourself to the church. I'll take care of the German people." Niemöller replied, "You said, 'I will take care of the German people.' But we too, as Christians and churchmen, have a responsibility toward the German people. That responsibility was entrusted to us by God, and neither you nor anyone in this world has the power to take it from us." Hitler listened in silence, but that evening his Gestapo raided Niemöller's rectory, and a few days later a bomb exploded in his church.

During the months and years following, Niemöller was closely watched by the secret police. Conflict was rising, and it was obvious that widespread war was coming. Niemöller remained peaceful despite his knowledge that he was in constant danger. In June 1937, he preached these words to his church: "We have no more thought of using our own powers to escape the arm of the authorities than had the apostles of old. We must obey God rather than man." He was soon arrested and placed in solitary confinement.

Niemöller's trial began on February 7, 1938. That morning, a uniformed guard escorted this courageous pastor from his prison cell and through a series of underground passages toward the courtroom. Niemöller was filled with fear. In prison, his loneliness was oppressive. What was going to happen to him? His family? His church? What tortures awaited them all?

The guard did not speak. His face was stonily impassive. But as they exited a tunnel to ascend a final flight of stairs, Niemöller heard a whisper. At first he didn't know where it came from, for the voice was very soft and barely audible. Then he realized that the officer was breathing into his ear the words of Proverbs 18:10: "The LORD is a mighty tower where his people can run for safety" (CEV). Niemöller's fear fell away, and the power of that verse sustained him through his trial and his years in Nazi concentration camps.[1]

Our Lord Jesus is the mighty tower that gives us peace. He is the mighty tower that the world can't compare or compete.

Reflecting and Recording

The following are designations of the peace Christ gives. Reflect on each of them, and make some notes on your most recent experience of each. How has peace in each of these areas come?

The peace of a clear conscience.

The time I did what was right instead of what a friend wanted me to do. It cost me the friendship but I knew it was what God was telling me to do. I still pray for my lost friend.

The peace of forgiveness.

Knowing I am forgiven when my witness to one I have been praying for is less bold than it should be. Knowing I can pray for more strength at the next opportunity and will receive it.

The peace of quiet acceptance.

When my mother died, knowing she was having her prayer to go home answered. Knowing she was reunited with those who had gone ahead in the presence of God.

The peace of God's presence.

When the news comes on and it seems that chaos reigns more every day, just knowing that He still has it in His hands and that understanding it all is not my job, only trusting, following and obeying with all the ability I have.

During the Day

Live today in the peace of God's presence. You can provide for others the peace of forgiveness and the peace of quiet acceptance. Offer that peace to at least one person today.

Being Reminded

"All this I have spoken while still with you. But the Advocate, the Holy Spirit, whom the Father will send in my name, will teach you all things and will remind you of everything I have said to you."

—JOHN 14:25–26

I was flattered a few years ago when Janice Grana and Charla Honea, editors of the *Upper Room*, asked me to go through my writings and glean some truths expressed in a sentence or two. They wanted me to provide something that might capture the mind and heart of people and give them something to chew on. They said today it might be described as a collection of tweets.

Someone suggested, tongue in cheek I'm sure, that it might be called "Maxie's Maxims" but we all knew that wouldn't do. I began to think about my preaching and my communication style. I seek by repetition to plant a truth firmly in the mind of listeners. Many times, when I state a truth and really want it to sink in, I use the phrase, "Let me say that again."

So that's what we called the book: *Let Me Say That Again.* What better thing can I ever do than simply say again what the Christian faith is all about—to rehearse the essence of the gospel, and tell the old story of Jesus and His love?

Jesus promised us the Holy Spirit who would be sent in His name, to "remind you of everything I have said to you" (v. 26). Jesus knew we constantly needed to be reminded. Even in the last few hours He had with His disciples He said many things more than once. It was as though He was saying, "Let me say that again." He promised the Holy Spirit, sent in His name, to "remind you of everything I have said to you."

Let's look at one of the important things He said to us more than once. We consider it again because it is so important: God loves you. "Let me say that again," Jesus would say. God loves you. In fact, God loves you as though you were the only person in the world to love. We have that on the authority of Scripture. This is the golden thread that runs through the Bible. Consider Psalm 8, which I shared on Day One of this week: "When I consider thy heavens, the work of thy fingers, the moon and the stars, which thou hast ordained; What is man, that thou art mindful of him? and the son of man, that thou visitest him? For thou has made him a little lower than the angels, and hast crowned him with glory and honour" (vv. 3–5 KJV). The birth of stars and galaxies . . . creation alone was not enough; creatures for relationship were essential for God's being. So we're the pinnacle of creation, made in God's image, and God loves us.

One of the most haunting words in the Old Testament that captures this is Isaiah's record of God speaking of His people, Israel: "Can a mother forget the baby at her breast and have no compassion on the child she has borne? Though she may forget, I will not forget you! See, I have engraved you on the palms of my hands . . ." (Isa. 49:15–16).

And the ultimate expression, of course, is John 3:16: "For God so loved the world that he gave his one and only Son, that whoever believes in him shall not perish but have eternal life." It's the golden thread that runs through the entire Bible. God loves you. That means at least three things: (1) you are special, (2) you have access to the Father, and (3) you can be forgiven.

Focus for a moment on the third. Nothing is more important for us to know: we can be forgiven. Let me say that again. God loves you; you can be forgiven. This is no superficial religious expression of the psychological dictum, "I'm okay, you're okay." This is the profound expression of the heart of the gospel. I chose my words deliberately. I was tempted to say, "You are forgiven." I deliberately said, "You *can be* forgiven." There is a difference. God's forgiveness is a fact. The cross is God's great act of love and forgiveness. But to appropriate that requires something of us. The demand of repentance is laid upon us—deep grief and sorrow for our sin. As the liturgy for Holy Communion puts it, there must be an intention to "lead a new life by following the commandments of God."

When we know that we're loved by God and when we know that God's ultimate act of love is to forgive us—if we know that in our heart of hearts—we are driven to repentance. Repentance flows out of gratitude for what God has done for us and the opportunity that can be ours to find and live a new life, free of sin and guilt.

The most thrilling experiences of my ten-year presidency of Asbury Theological Seminary were our worship services on Tuesdays and Thursdays. Estes Chapel would be full of students and faculty for our worship together. The singing was glorious. Many times we would have testimonies.

During "Senior Week" at the beginning of May, we had chapel every day. Seniors planned the services. In every chapel we not only had a student who did the preaching, we had at least one testimony. I never will forget the testimony of one young man. All of his adult life—until he was twenty-seven—he had practiced a homosexual lifestyle. He told of his pain and guilt, his anguish as he struggled with what he called his distorted sexual lust. He told of his deliverance, expressing appreciation for a church that acted as a transforming congregation in his life; of twelve-step programs that had tremendous meaning, especially in terms of support and acceptance. But then he made this powerful statement, "It was not until I accepted the love of Christ, and repented, that I was loosed from the power of my homosexual lust."

He left that lifestyle, answered the call to preach, spent four years in theological training, and was appointed as a pastor of a local congregation. The congregations he has served have been fortunate, because their pastor is able to talk firsthand about the love of God, a love which forgives and transforms—a love that has the power to break every shackle that binds us.

Let me say it again: God loves you. You're special, you have access to the Father, and you can be forgiven.

Reflecting and Recording

Make enough notes here to get in touch with your experience when you first became aware of the fact that you were truly loved by God.

Forgiveness is not a one-time experience. Is there something for which you need the forgiveness of another and/or God? Deal with that now by facing it honestly, confessing to God, genuinely repenting, and receiving God's forgiveness.

During the Day

If you need the forgiveness of another, share your confession and desire for forgiveness with that person today. If you cannot do that personally, call or write them. It is important that you act on this in the present awareness of your need to be forgiven.

As you move through the day, stay alert to the persons with whom you share. There will likely come an occasion for you to remind someone that God loves them. Do that with joy and in the confidence that God loves you.

DAY FIVE

Jesus' Dual Invitation

"I am the true vine, and my Father is the gardener. He cuts off every branch in me that bears no fruit, while every branch that does bear fruit he prunes so that it will be even more fruitful. You are already clean because of the word I have spoken to you. Remain in me, as I also remain in you. No branch can bear fruit by itself; it must remain in the vine. Neither can you bear fruit unless you remain in me.

"I am the vine; you are the branches. If you remain in me and I in you, you will bear much fruit; apart from me you can do nothing."

—John 15:1–5

Jesus extended a dual invitation: (1) come unto Me and (2) abide in Me and I will abide in you. The first invitation is a call *to* Christ, to accept Him as Savior; the second is the ongoing call to discipleship . . . not just *to come*, but *to remain*, to abide in Christ.

In this suggestive image of the vine, Jesus tells us who God is and who He is in relation to God: "I am the true vine, and my Father is the gardener" (v. 1). Then He tells us who we are in relation to Him: "I am the vine; you are the branches" (v. 5).

Jesus uses this vine/branch image to call us to "remain" (abide) in Him. The picture suggests resting in Christ, finding our strength and comfort in Him. It suggests growing, being nurtured by His presence with us. It also suggests action, service, discipleship: "If you remain in me and I in you, you will bear much fruit" (v. 5). Accountability and judgment are also here: "apart from me you can do nothing. If you do not remain in me, you are like a branch that is thrown away and withers" (vv. 5–6).

Perhaps the best way to appropriate the rich meaning here and the core message of John 15 is to focus on that awesome truth in verse 16: "You did not choose me, but I chose you." The comic strip *Pogo* helps us here. *Pogo* was the title and central character of the long-running daily American comic strip, created by cartoonist Walt Kelly. It was set in the Okefenokee Swamp of the southeastern United States, and often engaged in social and political satire, with challenging effectiveness. Many times, the cartoon set my mind thinking of spiritual matters.

I remember one sequence that went something like this: a duck comes up to Pogo who is on the riverbank, fishing. "Howdy, Pogo," the duck says, "Is you seen my cousin?"

"Your cousin?" Pogo asks.

"Yes," says the duck. "He's migratin' north by kiddy-car."

"A duck migrating by a kiddy-car?" asks Pogo.

"Yes," replies the duck. "He is affeared to fly, affeared he might fall off."

Pogo asks, "Why doesn't he swim?"

The duck answers, "He gets seasick."

Pogo, pondering the duck's strange cousin, shakes his head and declares, "All I can say is that when he decided to be a duck, he picked the wrong business."

This is what Jesus is telling us. We didn't "pick our business" of being Christian. "You did not choose me, but I chose you" (John 15:16).

We have not chosen God; God has chosen us. In His extravagant grace, He has given us His love, and confronted us with His call.

One of the most unforgettable times of my life was the Fifteenth World Methodist Conference in Nairobi, South Africa, in July 1986, of which I was privileged to be the program chair. The highlights were numerous. For me, the most electric and meaningful was the testimony of Peter Storey, a white Methodist preacher who was serving in Johannesburg.

Storey began his testimony:

I want you to celebrate with me and with my sisters and brothers from South Africa that at the heart of our faith there is one astounding paradox. If you want to know whether God is alive, don't go to the places of comfort and ease; inquire rather in those places where the fire of testing burns hottest. Living in the furnace of apartheid forges a unique experience of God. It melts away cheap piety, until all that is left is something you know is real—Someone you know is real. That there is in that furnace with you another whose form is like that of the Son of God.[1]

This is the testimony of Jesus over and over again as He shares those last hours with His disciples—that He is with us, always and in every circumstance. We'll reflect more on this the next couple of days.

Reflecting and Recording

In preaching and teaching you have experienced, has the dual invitation been balanced? Have you heard, "Abide in me," as much as, "Come unto me"? Think about that for a few minutes. Where has been the greater emphasis? Why do you think that is so?

I believe they are balanced in our church. If "come unto me" has been stressed more in some places, I think it is because the speakers think those who are abiding without first coming, but

To what degree, and in what ways, do you practice *abiding* in Christ? *that abiding will naturally follow coming eventually. I try to begin each day with Bible reading and prayer for guidance. If for some reason I don't have a chance at the start of the day, I try to make a time later.*

Peter Storey's testimony about the presence of God in the struggle with oppressive apartheid is a dramatic one. Few of our experiences are that dramatic, yet most of us have experienced the Presence in difficult situations. Recall your most recent experience of knowing that God was with you. Briefly describe that experience here.

During the Day

Testimony is the convincing evidence people need to hear. Find the occasion today to share with someone the experience you have described.

Chosen for Privilege

"As the Father has loved me, so have I loved you. Now remain in my love. If you keep my commands, you will remain in my love, just as I have kept my Father's commands and remain in his love. I have told you this so that my joy may be in you and that your joy may be complete."

—John 15:9–11

Back in 1981, the attention of the world was focused on the wedding of Prince Charles and Lady Diana. My wife, an almost hopeless romantic, became emotionally involved in that event. We were traveling when the wedding took place, and I remember she stayed up almost all night in a hotel room where we were, watching the live television broadcast. She also read all the newspaper accounts, and she even gave our two daughters beautiful color picture albums that recaptured this wedding of the decade.

Because she read all the newspaper accounts, she was constantly feeding me with different aspects of what was taking place, and I remember vividly one newspaper report. The reporter was describing the arrival of the entourage at the cathedral where the wedding was to take place. He noted how all the royal family were carried in special royal coaches, while Lady Diana arrived in the coach of a commoner. Then there was this rather telling sentence: "Lady Diana came to the church as a commoner; she departed as royalty."

This is a vivid description of what grace is all about. We come as sinners, but grace turns us into heirs and joint heirs with Christ of all that God wants to give us. It also is a vivid description of the possibility that comes to each one of us—the possibility of a deeper walk with Christ.

Jesus said to His disciples, "You did not choose me, but I chose you" (John 15:16). We have not chosen God; God has chosen us. In His extravagant grace, He has given us His love, and confronted us with His call. We arrive in His presence as commoners; we leave as royalty.

This is our privilege. It is the privilege of an intimate, ongoing relationship. And this relationship is the source of joy. "I have told you this so that my joy may be in you and that your joy may be complete" (v. 11).

The Greek word for "joy" is *chara*. It is related to the word *charis*, which is the Greek word for "grace." It has about it a sense of surprise and excitement. It isn't earned; it is a gift—thus the connection with grace. We will think more about this on Day Four of next week.

Back to the basic claim: having been chosen by Christ is the privilege of an intimate, ongoing relationship. This relationship flavors all of life. There is an old hymn by Robert Wadsworth Lowry that captures this, even in its title, "How Can I Keep from Singing?"

My life flows on in endless song;
Above earth's lamentation,
I hear the sweet, tho' far-off hymn
That hails a new creation;
Thro' all the tumult and the strife
I hear the music ringing;
It finds an echo in my soul—
How can I keep from singing?

I know that I am made a new person by accepting His grace and love.

What tho' my joys and comforts die?
The Lord my Saviour liveth;
What tho' the darkness gather round?
Songs in the night he giveth.
No storm can shake my inmost calm
While to that refuge clinging;
Since Christ is Lord of heaven and earth,
How can I keep from singing?

No matter what circumstances happen to me, I can be happy knowing He is in charge no matter what it seems to be.

I lift my eyes; the cloud grows thin;
I see the blue above it;
And day by day this pathway smooths,
Since first I learned to love it,
The peace of Christ makes fresh my heart,
A fountain ever springing;
All things are mine since I am his—
How can I keep from singing?

Knowing He is with me always makes it possible to find peace even in chaos.

Reflecting and Recording

Use the highlighted lines in the hymn to help you reflect on the privilege of being chosen by Christ. Begin by reading again the first stanza of the hymn, let the affirmation settle in your mind and heart, then beside the highlighted lines, in your own words make your own statement, saying in your own way what the writer has said. Do the same with each of the stanzas.

During the Day

Move through the day, claiming "all things are mine since I am his," and see how many times you can acclaim, "How can I keep from singing?"

Chosen for Partnership

"I no longer call you servants, because a servant does not know his master's business. Instead, I have called you friends, for everything that I learned from my Father I have made known to you. You did not choose me, but I chose you and appointed you so that you might go and bear fruit—fruit that will last—and so that whatever you ask in my name the Father will give you."

—John 15:15–16

R ead now the way Paul captured Jesus' claim that we are loved and that He has chosen us.

The Spirit you received does not make you slaves, so that you live in fear again; rather, the Spirit you received brought about your adoption to sonship. And by him we cry, "*Abba*, Father." The Spirit himself testifies with our spirit that we are God's children. Now if we are children, then we are heirs—heirs of God and co-heirs with Christ, if indeed we share in his sufferings in order that we may also share in his glory. (Rom. 8:15–17)

The title "slave" or "servant" of God is not a title of shame; it was indeed a title of the highest honor. Moses was the servant, the slave of God (see Deuteronomy 34:5); so was Joshua (see Joshua 24:29), and so was David (see Psalm 89:20).

It was a title that Paul counted an honor to use (see Titus 1:1). Over and over again, he was proud to address himself, "Paul, a servant [slave] of Jesus Christ." The disciples knew this, that the greatest men in the past had been called the *slaves of God*. How they must have quivered inside when Jesus said, "I have something greater for you yet: you are no longer slaves; you are My friends" (author's paraphrase).

In the culture of the time, the slave could never be a partner. The slave was defined in Greek law as a living tool. His master never opened his mind to him. The slave had to do what he was told without reason and without explanation. But Jesus said to us, "I no longer call you servants, because a servant does not know his master's business. Instead, I have called you friends, for everything that I learned from my Father I have made known to you" (John 15:15). Are you listening? Jesus is saying, "I have told you what I am trying to do, and why I am trying to do it." Jesus has given us the honor of making us His partners in His kingdom enterprise. He has shared His mind with us, and opened His heart to us.[1]

Are you listening? What does it mean to be partners with Christ?

Too much of what the church does, I am afraid, emphasizes our privilege. Forty times in John's Gospel alone, Jesus mentions the importance of our being sent. As He was sent by the Father, He sends us.

Jesus was always going out in the sense that He was always seeking and serving people who had not yet experienced being chosen as friends of God. You can't read the New Testament without realizing that. The Lord dined with Pharisees and Publicans. He shocked people by going home with Zacchaeus. He shocked them even more by paying attention to an adulteress. He simply didn't seem to have refused invitations to share hospitality in whatever quarter it came.

The legalistic Pharisees complained that he was "a glutton and a drunkard, a friend of tax collectors and sinners" (Luke 7:34). A part of that is true. He was not gluttonous, He was not a winebibber, but He was a friend of the Publicans and sinners.

Focus on that for a moment. Jesus' mission was always to minister at the point of whatever need He discovered. We have to keep learning that lesson over and over again in the church. It never seems to stay with us.

A friend of mine, Sir Alan Walker, told of having a preaching mission in Florida. The church was packed with people, and after the evening service had begun, a man—unshaven, somewhat dirty, a cigarette hanging from his mouth—wandered into the side door of the church at the front of the sanctuary. He stood there simply observing what was going on.

He made no noise, caused no commotion, but certainly got a lot of attention. He leaned up against the wall, and began to listen and look. Very soon ushers came up and engaged him in quiet conversation, and it wasn't long before quietly and without adieu they were accompanying him out the door.

After the service, a very proper and polite woman, handsomely dressed, wanted to make sure that Sir Alan had not been distracted or upset by what had gone on. She asked him if he had seen the man come in and all that went on. She concluded by saying, "He obviously knew that he didn't belong here."

What a pity! If anyone belonged there, it probably was that particular man.

Our city, Memphis, is a very troubled city. It has been designated as the third most dangerous city of its size in the nation. Crime rages. Poverty takes its toll on families, and the deep racial divide flavors everything we do. We are a very troubled city. Yet, I don't know another city that has as many churches committed to the common good, and faith-based groups who are committed to the welfare of our city. I travel, and am in touch with church life across the nation, especially the mainline and evangelical Protestant expressions, and I don't know a city that has more creative expressions of mission and ministry as we have in Memphis.

Even so, we don't seem to get traction for transformation. But I believe it is coming; it's coming because we have grasped the truth that *the grace of God is so radical that, when we express it in its fullness, those around us may think we are accepting the lifestyles and sins of the people we seek to serve.*

With that thought tumbling around in your mind, I challenge us to measure our partnership with Jesus by responding to the following questions.

Who are the people in our community who have yet to receive a clear message from you and your church that you deeply care for them and that God loves them?

What about the recovering community, those folks seeking freedom from alcohol and drugs? Are you and your community of faith a place of welcome, a place of grace that will help them break the chains of shame and blame?

What about the thousands of children in your city who don't yet have access to a good educational opportunity? A child's zip code should not determine his or her opportunity for education.

What about the immigrants in your community? Are you and your community of faith showing hospitality to these strangers in our midst, those who are culturally homeless? We have spent millions of dollars in the past going to them in faithfulness to the Great Commission. Now they are coming to us. Is the Great Commission still operative? Remember that word from Hebrews 13:2: "In welcoming these strangers, we may be entertaining angels unawares" (author's paraphrase).

Reflecting and Recording

In the last four paragraphs above, four groups are mentioned: those desperately needing to know they are loved by us and by God, the recovering community, children needing education, and immigrants. Read those paragraphs again, and be honest in assessing how you and/or your community of faith are responding to and reaching these folks with the love of Christ.

During the Day

Select one of the four groups to think about as you move through the day, committing yourself to making some sort of effort to share love or concern. It may be a phone call of encouragement to a person you know is struggling with his or her recovery, or a ministry with immigrants that needs your encouragement and support.

GROUP MEETING FOR WEEK FOUR

• INTRODUCTION •

Paul advised the Philippians to "let your conversation be as it becometh the gospel" (Phil. 1:27 KJV). Most of us have yet to see the dynamic potential of the conversation that takes place in an intentional group such as this. The Elizabethan word for *life* as used in the King James Version is *conversation,* thus Paul's word to the Philippians. Life is found in communion with God and also in conversation with others.

Speaking and listening with this sort of deep meaning that communicates life is not easy. This week we have listened to Jesus talk about being chosen by God. When we really listen to Jesus, we are called to respond, and responding often means submission. The principle also holds in our conversation with others. When we listen in a way that makes a difference, we surrender ourselves to the other person, saying, "I will hear what you have to say and will receive you as I receive your words." When we speak in a way that makes a difference, we speak for the sake of others; thus we are serving.

In this sharing and in the following weeks we have together, listen to others in the fashion of listening to Jesus—in a way of response and submission.

• SHARING TOGETHER •

1. Invite someone to read aloud Psalm 8:3–5, printed on Day One of this week. Now spend ten to fifteen minutes discussing the claim: "There is a place in God's heart that only you can fill."
2. Did anyone have any problem with the claim, "We trust Jesus with some things, some of the time, when we need to trust Him with all things all the time"? Discuss this for a few minutes.
3. Invite someone to read aloud John 14:12–14.

Now spend ten to fifteen minutes discussing the two fantastic promises Jesus gives us: "Greater things than I have done will you do" and "Whatever you ask, if you believe, I will do." In your discussion, press each other with the question: How are these promises being worked out in your life?

4. Invite a couple of people to share an experience when they attempted something so great for God they knew they would fail unless they were empowered by the Holy Spirit.

5. On Day Three you were asked to reflect and record experiences of peace. Ask someone to share his or her experience of peace that came from a clear conscience; the peace of forgiveness; the peace of quiet acceptance; or the peace of God's presence

6. Spend the rest of your time discussing what it means to be chosen by God. What questions do you have about being chosen? How are you working out for what purpose you have been chosen?

• PRAYING TOGETHER •

As we have been insisting, corporate prayer is one of the great blessings of the Christian community. To affirm that is one thing; to *experience* it is another. To experience it we have to *experiment* with the possibility. While Jesus insisted that being alone with God is a basic dimension of prayer, we need to understand also the possibility of the mind and will of God becoming clear to us when we pray with others. "If two of you on earth agree . . ." (Matt. 18:19).

Will you become a bit bolder now, and experiment with the possibilities of corporate prayer by sharing more opening and intimately?

Leaders, keep time now.

1. Spend three minutes in quietness, asking yourself, *Do I really believe there is a place in God's heart that only I can fill? What is hindering me from believing that?*

2. Invite as many as will to share one barrier to their believing that there is a place in God's heart that only they can fill. (Participants may want to take notes so they can pray for their friends in a more focused way.)

3. There is a sense in which, through this sharing, you have already been corporately praying. There is power, however, in a community on a common journey verbalizing thoughts and feelings to God in the presence of fellow pilgrims. In a time of corporate prayer, think of the persons who have shared, and have someone offer a brief verbal prayer for particular persons and/or concerns. Make sure that every person who has shared a hindrance in believing that there is a place in God's heart that only he/she can fill is named and prayed for.

4. When the leader senses the mentioned needs have been responded to, simply close the praying with this word, "In the name of the Father who created us and loves us, and the Son who in love redeemed us, and the Holy Spirit present with us to empower and guide, amen."

Joy in Relationship with Christ

In Christ

"I will not leave you desolate; I will come to you. . . . and he who loves me will be loved by my Father . . . and we [the Father and I] will come to him and make our home with him."

JOHN 14:18, 21, 23 RSV

For this reason I kneel before the Father, from whom every family in heaven and on earth derives its name. I pray that out of his glorious riches he may strengthen you with power through his Spirit in your inner being, so that Christ may dwell in your hearts through faith. And I pray that you, being rooted and established in love, may have power, together with all the Lord's holy people, to grasp how wide and long and high and deep is the love of Christ, and to know this love that surpasses knowledge—that you may be filled to the measure of all the fullness of God.

Now to him who is able to do immeasurably more than all we ask or imagine, according to his power that is at work within us, to him be glory in the church and in Christ Jesus throughout all generations, for ever and ever! Amen.

—EPHESIANS 3:14–21

Paul championed two great concepts of the Christian faith: justification by grace through faith and the indwelling Christ. Protestant Christianity has done a good job in proclaiming and teaching justification—that is, how to become a Christian. But we have done a very poor job helping people become full-blown disciples of Jesus Christ. We too often concentrate on conversion—getting people saved—but fail at growing people up as mature Christ-followers.

Paul wrote his autobiography in two sentences: "I have been crucified with Christ and I no longer live, but Christ lives in me. The life I now live in the body, I live by faith in the Son of God, who loved me and gave himself for me" (Gal. 2:20). That's an extravagant claim. We could pass it off and not pay too much attention to it if this was an isolated instance in his witness and writing. But this is the language Paul uses throughout his letters.

"In Christ," "in union with Christ," "Christ in you"—these are recurring phrases in Paul's vocabulary. Variations of that phrase occur no less than 172 times in the New Testament. Paul's definition of a Christian is a person in Christ: "If any one is in Christ, he is a new creation; the old has passed away, behold, the new has come" (2 Cor. 5:17 RSV).

Certainly we must not diminish the foundation of our Christian experience, that we are justified by grace through faith. I believe, however, that what is glaringly missing is the conviction and confidence that we can live our lives, daily, *in Christ*, and reflect His likeness in the world.

Jesus' promise, when He was talking to His disciples about His death, was the clear sounding of this dynamic of the indwelling Christ. How they must have puzzled over His word: "I will not leave you desolate; I will come to you. . . . and he who loves me will be loved by my Father . . . and we [the Father and I] will come to him and make our home with him" (John 14:18, 21, 23 RSV). Wow!

I hope your mind and heart quivers as mine as you hear that, "[The Father and I] will come to [you] and make our home in [you]." The resurrection gave the disciples hope and confirmed the victory of the cross for our salvation. But it was not until Pentecost that the meaning of the promise became clear.

Stanley Jones made the observation that the "in Christ" language that is dominant in Paul's writing is not found in the Synoptic Gospels—Matthew, Mark, and Luke. The stage of those Gospels as related to Jesus was "Immanuel . . . God *with* us, but not *in us.*" The account says that Jesus chose twelve "to be *with* him" (Mark 3:14 RSV, author's emphasis). They were *with* Him, but not *in* Him. The "in Him" stage comes after the coming of the Holy Spirit at Pentecost. Up to then, it was "with" and, after that, "in." The "with" had to end that the "in" might begin. He withdrew His presence and gave them His omnipresence.[1]

Paul was giving dramatic expression to the promise of Jesus that was fulfilled in the resurrection. Tomorrow, we will consider how this connects with Jesus' claim, "I am the vine; you are the branches" (John 15:5).

Reflecting and Recording

Sit quietly and imagine Jesus is sitting with you. However you envision Him, see Him sitting there. Read these words aloud as Jesus speaks them to you: "I will not leave you desolate; I will come to you. . . . and he who loves me will be loved by my Father . . . and we [the Father and I] will come to him and make our home with him" (John 14:18, 21, 23 RSV).

Repeat the exercise, letting Jesus speak to you.

You love Jesus; you know that. What does it feel like now to hear Jesus say, "he who loves me will be loved by my Father" (John 14:23 RSV)? Settle into the conviction that you are loved by the Creator, the Sovereign of the universe.

During the Day

One of the most amazing passages of Scripture in the entire Bible is Jesus' promise, "[The Father and I] will come to [you] and make our home with [you]" (John 14:23 RSV). Recall it as many times as possible today, saying aloud to yourself, "Jesus promised that He and the Father would come and make their home in me."

The Fullness of God's Presence

"I am the true vine, and my Father is the gardener. He cuts off every branch in me that bears no fruit, while every branch that does bear fruit he prunes so that it will be even more fruitful. You are already clean because of the word I have spoken to you. Remain in me, as I also remain in you. No branch can bear fruit by itself; it must remain in the vine. Neither can you bear fruit unless you remain in me.

"I am the vine; you are the branches. If you remain in me and I in you, you will bear much fruit; apart from me you can do nothing."

—JOHN 15:1–5

I pray that out of his glorious riches he may strengthen you with power through his Spirit in your inner being, so that Christ may dwell in your hearts through faith. And I pray that you, being rooted and established in love, may have power, together with all the Lord's holy people, to grasp how wide and long and high and deep is the love of Christ, and to know this love that surpasses knowledge—that you may be filled to the measure of all the fullness of God.

—EPHESIANS 3:16–19

Jesus introduced Himself in different ways; in a number of ways, making "I am" claims: I am the door (see John 10:7), the good shepherd (see John 10:11), the way, truth, light (see John 14:6), the bread of life (see John 6:35). Here, during His last meal with His disciples, He makes the claim, "I am the vine." Though we reflected on this on Day Five of last week, we need to continue that reflection.

This was a familiar image with which His listeners could readily identify. Palestine was vineyard country, and grapes were the common fruit of the land. The disciples knew about the vine and branches, about fruit bearing and pruning, about dead branches being burned.

But not only so because, as Jews, these disciples knew the vine as the symbol of Israel. Over and over again in the Old Testament, Israel is pictured as the vine or the vineyard of God. "The vineyard of the LORD of hosts is the house of Israel" (Isa. 5:7 RSV). "I planted you [Israel] a choice vine" (Jer. 2:21 RSV). The prophet Hosea spoke it as a word of judgment: "Israel is an empty vine" (Hos. 10:1 KJV). Thinking of God's deliverance of His people from bondage, the psalmist sang, "You transplanted a vine from Egypt" (Ps. 80:8).

As Jews, the disciples knew themselves to be a part of Israel, this vine of God whose roots stemmed from Abraham, Isaac, and Jacob. They were a part of a chosen race, which made Jesus' word, "You did not choose me, but I chose you" (John 15:16), even more mysterious and challenging. They were not sure what it was all about, nor were they unshakably sure about why they were following Him. And what was Jesus saying, "Abide in me" (John 15:4 RSV)?

We continue our thinking about the *indwelling Christ*. Did it sink into your mind and heart as you repeated it often yesterday? "[The Father and I] will come to [you] and make our home with [you]" (John 14:23 RSV).

The resurrection gave the disciples hope and confirmed the victory of the cross for our salvation. But it was not until Pentecost that the meaning of the promise became clear. So, Paul prayed that the promise of the indwelling Christ would be fulfilled in the Ephesians 3:14–21.

Is your mind open? Is your heart ready . . . *"that Christ may dwell in your [heart] through faith"* (Eph. 3:17, author's emphasis). Get that, Christ dwelling in our hearts. . . *"that you may be filled to the measure of all the fullness of God"* (Eph. 3:19, author's emphasis). Outrageous! On the surface, unbelievable for most. How can it be? You, me, any one of us, *filled with the fullness of God.* Living a life in Christ is our calling and privilege.

Reflecting and Recording

Read slowly and reflectively Paul's prayer for the Ephesians quoted at the beginning of this day.

If we respond to Jesus' invitation, "Abide in me and I will abide in you," isn't Paul's prayer being answered? *That Christ may dwell in your [heart] through faith . . . that you may be filled to the measure of all the fullness of God"* (Eph. 3:17, 19, author's emphasis).

Now close your time of reflection by thinking, *Paul was not only praying that prayer for the Ephesians, he could have been praying it for all that came after him, including me.* To what degree and in what way is that prayer being answered in your life?

During the Day

We discipline ourselves to abide in Christ. One of the ways we do that is by cultivating awareness of His presence. So continue today recalling as many times as possible, Jesus' promise: "[The Father and I] will come to [you] and make our home with [you]" (John 14:23 RSV). Say aloud, "Jesus promised that He and the Father would come and make their home in me."

Apart from Me

> "Abide in me, and I in you. As the branch cannot bear fruit by itself, unless it abides in the vine, neither can you, unless you abide in me. I am the vine, you are the branches. He who abides in me, and I in him, he it is that bears much fruit, for apart from me you can do nothing. If a man does not abide in me, he is cast forth as a branch and withers; and the branches are gathered, thrown into the fire and burned."
>
> —JOHN 15:4–6 RSV

It may not be obvious in the imagery, but certainly implicit here is God's care of the vineyard. Jesus is the *true* vine, and His Father owns the vineyard and cares for it. As with any responsible vineyard owner, God's primary purpose is for the vineyard to bear fruit. It is the branches, not the vine, that bears fruit. So the branches that do not bear fruit are taken away. When they become dry and lifeless, they are cast out and burned.

This is the final judgment on those who do not *abide* in the vine. They once flourished and bore fruit, but the Source of life was cut off, and now they are dead. Even as Jesus was lovingly sharing with His closest followers, Judas was planning his betrayal. Also, in the larger religious arena of the Jews, the synagogue, once the center of faith, had become legalistic and hard. It can happen to us as well. Disregard for truth, selfish interest, unconfessed sin, and an unforgiving spirit block the flow of life from the Vine to the branches. Gradually the branch dies, and is taken away and burned as trash.

Take note. The Father is the *vinedresser* who prunes the sprouts and leaves that would hinder the branches from bearing fruit. The fruit-bearing branches must get all the nourishment; little shoots that take life from the vine are cut off. This pruning is the Vinedresser's discipline, His call for us to rearrange our time and priorities, to cast aside peripheral interests, to disallow the sprouts of troubles, disappointments, and defeats to take energy from our fruit-bearing calling.

Two big words glare out from this passage: *abide* and *apart*. Unlike abide, there is nothing soothing in the word "apart." In fact, it is a harsh, painful word. There is a kind of finality about it, "apart from me you can do nothing" (v. 5). It's difficult not to connect this with another finality word of Jesus in His parable of the last judgment in Matthew 25, "Depart from me" (v. 41).

Depart from me is a pronouncement of judgment that comes if we live our lives *apart from Christ*. We will be cast out as a branch that withers; we will be gathered and thrown into the fire and burned.

That's a frightening notion, so frightening that we give it too little thought. Judgment is written into the very fabric of life, and the Bible makes it clear that there will be a final judgment, and each of us will have to give an account before God.

Don't tell me God is too loving to condemn us. That misses the point. God is loving, and it is not God who condemns. Our judgment is implicit in our actions or failures to act. Jesus Christ is a loving friend and companion. He is Savior and wants to be Lord. He does everything, goes even to the limit of the cross, to graft each one of us to the Vine, that we might be sustained and saved.

The alternatives are ours: *abiding in Christ*, living and fruitful; *apart from Christ,* barren and destined to be cast aside.

Reflecting and Recording

Is it true that we think of judgment too seldom? When was the last time you heard a sermon on judgment? When was the last time you spent time alone, thinking about judgment or had a conversation with someone about judgment?

Spend a few minutes reflecting on the assertion that it is not God who condemns. Our condemnation is implicit in our actions or our failures to act.

Disregard for truth, selfish interest, unconfessed sin, and an unforgiving spirit were mentioned as forces that block the flow of life from the Vine to the branches. Look at those, put an "X" above any of those forces that may be present in your life.

Spend the rest of your time thinking about pruning. What does the Vinedresser need to prune from your life to make you more Christlike, and more fruit-bearing?

During the Day

Continue cultivating awareness of the indwelling Christ by seeking to recall as often as possible and repeating to yourself Jesus' word to you: "Apart from me you can do nothing" (John 15:5 RSV).

Joy in Obedience

"As the Father has loved me, so have I loved you; abide in my love. If you keep my commandments, you will abide in my love, just as I have kept my Father's commandments and abide in his love. These things I have spoken to you, that my joy may be in you, and that your joy may be full."

—John 15:9–11 RSV

G. K. Chesterton said that joy is "the gigantic secret of the Christian."[1] What does Chesterton mean? Isn't joy what the world offers on every hand? We've even named a dish-washing detergent Joy. But note the context of Jesus' promise of joy. He is teaching us that joy is the result, the by-product, of our obedience to Him. Our Scripture today builds on Jesus' allegory of the vine and the branches. As we, by faith and obedience, abide in Christ, we know, experience, and enjoy Jesus' love—and joy is the fruit of that branch which abides in the Vine.

Chesterton, then, is right: joy *is* the gigantic secret of the Christian. We have learned the source of joy—abiding in and obeying Christ. Authentic, lasting joy is a by-product of our obedience and discipline, our abiding in Christ.

The bottom line: you will enjoy your discipleship in proportion to your obedience.

This was not Jesus' only promise of joy. Chapter 16 of John's Gospel focuses almost entirely on joy. Jesus was talking about His coming death, and He said in verse 20: "Truly, truly, I say to you, you will weep and lament, but the world will rejoice; you will be sorrowful, but your sorrow will turn into joy" (RSV). Then He used the image of a woman in the travail and labor of childbirth. When she delivers her child, she forgets the pain and anguish because of the joy that is hers in her baby. Jesus closed that chapter with the promise: "These things I have spoken unto you, that in me ye might have peace. In the world ye shall have tribulation: but be of good cheer [be joyful]; I have overcome the world" (John 16:33 KJV).

No wonder Chesterton said joy is the gigantic secret of the Christian.

I have some dear friends, a clergy couple, who have gone through a very painful divorce. Clergy are human, and do crazy things just like other people. In my mind, this man lost his way. They had a thirty-year marriage, and had given their lives to Christ and His gospel.

I was visiting with my friend, the wife. You could feel, in a kind of alternating sort of way, tears in her voice as well as joy of her spirit. A thirty-year marriage doesn't end without taking its toll and without bringing almost unbearable trauma. She kept saying over and over again, "I'm going to make it."

At one point in our conversation, she talked about the way people would sometimes say to her, "His grace is sufficient for you." She would smile and nod, but beneath her breath she would say, "Barely, just barely." "But," she added to me, "that's all it takes—barely enough grace to be sufficient."

She concluded our conversation with something like this, "It would be a shame if I had heard and believed the gospel for this long and then gave it up or didn't trust it. I've embraced this event as tragedy, I've suffered in it, and am suffering through it, but I'm learning. And His grace *is* sufficient, though at times, *only barely*. Deep inside I have the joy of knowing who I am in relation to my Lord."

There it is: the joy of the Christian is that of the abiding presence of Christ. We enjoy our discipleship in proportion to our obedience. Our joy will never be taken away, and it will be complete.

Reflecting and Recording

You will enjoy your discipleship in proportion to your obedience. In what way have you found this claim true or not true?

Recall a trying experience, maybe a time of suffering, when you found God's grace sufficient, *but barely*. Make some notes here to bring that experience vividly in mind.

When Rebekah lost the quads, her third miscarriage. The last of seven grandchildren that I won't see until I get to heaven myself.

Thinking of that experience, though you might not have labeled it as such, was there joy in knowing God was caring for and sustaining you?

At the time I couldn't feel it. I still cry when that moment comes to mind. As time went on, I knew God was in it as in everything, that I would see them in eternity and be glad. Then we were blessed

During the Day
with Nick, and so thankful.

Memorize this word, repeat it often, and make it a reality today: "To live in joy is to live this *now* day of resurrection."

DAY FIVE

Chosen for Friendship

"My command is this: Love each other as I have loved you. Greater love has no one than this: to lay down one's life for one's friends. You are my friends if you do what I command. I no longer call you servants, because a servant does not know his master's business. Instead, I have called you friends, for everything that I learned from my Father I have made known to you."

—JOHN 15:12–15

Let your mind stand on tip-toe as you read, remembering that Jesus is speaking to you, even as He spoke to His disciples in the upper room.

"You did not choose me, but I chose you" (John 15:16).

How is that so? We return to our consideration of being chosen by Christ. Again, listen to Jesus and let His word sink into your mind and heart:

"As the Father has loved me, so have I loved you" (John 15:9).

Could there be a greater privilege, to be chosen by Christ? And the privilege is summed up gloriously by Jesus, "I no longer call you servants, because a servant does not know his master's business. Instead, I have called you friends, for everything I learned from my Father I have made known to you" (John 15:15).

Do you need to take a deep breath now? What privilege to be friends of Christ!

Since that may not touch us as deeply as it should, we need to rehearse the setting and know how tenderly piercing this word would have been for those who heard it.

The more precise translation here is, "No longer do I call you slaves." The Greek word is *doulos*. William Barclay reminds us that the title "the *doulas* of God"[1] was no title of shame;

it was indeed a title of the highest honor. As indicated earlier, Moses was the *doulos*, the servant, the slave of God (see Deuteronomy 34:5); so was Joshua (see Joshua 24:29); so was David (see Psalm 89:20). It is a title that Paul counted an honor to use (see Titus 1:1). Over and over again, he proudly addressed himself, "Paul, a servant [slave] of Jesus Christ."

> The greatest men in the past had been proud to be called the douloi, the slaves of God. And Jesus says: "I have something greater for you yet: you are no longer slaves; you are friends." Christ offers an intimacy with God which not even the greatest men and women knew before he came into the world.[2]

One of our greatest problems as Christians is that we forget that we are friends of Jesus. We seem unable to sustain the awareness of our identity. We allow the experience of God's love to become a vague hint of memory—no aliveness at all. The questions are: How do we keep the experience alive? How do we keep the vision of who we are, friends of Christ, glowing and growing in our lives?

One, we need to immerse ourselves in the witness of Scripture. The overwhelming message of Scripture is that God really loves His people—that we are friends of Christ. Scripture affirms it over and over again—that God loves us—and that His love reaches out to us, not as we might be if we were better, but that He loves us as we are and where we are.

Isaiah uses an emotion-laden image to picture God's love: "Can a mother forget her own baby and not love the child she bore? Even if a mother should forget her child, I will not forget you" (Isa. 49:15 TEV).

Jesus spoke of that love over and over in symbol and parable, the most unforgettable one being about a prodigal son. The grandeur of the story is revealed when the son, from the sheer motive of survival, decides to return home. The father is there, waiting and ready to receive him. When you distill that parable down to its most precious essence, it is this: when the prodigal returned home, the father received him as though he had never been away.

My favorite way of expressing it is: there is a place in God's heart that only you can fill, and God loves you as though you were the only person in the world to love.

So we need to immerse ourselves in Scripture to keep alive the awareness of who we are—friends of Christ.

Along with immersing ourselves in Scripture, memory is a source for staying alive to the love of God and our friendship with Christ.

The psalmists illustrated the power of memory. They talked about being "faint in their bones in agony" (6:2), "afflicted and in pain" (69:29), "cast down"(43:5 KJV), "like an owl of the waste places" (102:6 ESV), "caught in the snares of death" (116:3 RSV), and "eyes . . . weak with sorrow"(6:7), just to name a few. In the midst of cries of desolation and moans of despair, they emerged in joyous exaltation. The transition from sadness to song is memory, captured in a word like, "These things I remember as I pour out my soul: how I used to go to the house of God under the protection of the Mighty One" (42:4) or "I will remember the deeds of the LORD" (77:11).

It has been true for me. I can recall occasions when there was no doubt about it—God loves me and I am a friend of Christ: my conversion experience; the malignancy of my mother, in the midst of whose suffering the love of God sustained her and her family; a long period of recuperation following an auto accident that left me with a broken leg, broken ribs, and a punctured and collapsed lung; and sharing with my son in his long battle with addiction. They are all dramatic experiences, alive in my memory, which testify to my relationship with Christ.

Reflecting and Recording

Reflect on your present situation. Are you down? Are you feeling lonely and uncared for, like an owl of the waste places? Is your strength deleted, your zest for life nil? Are you having difficulty feeling the presence of God?

No.

Ponder your history, call to mind experiences that are clear witnesses of God's love. Live with those memories for a few minutes.

Spend what time you have now to allow this glorious truth to be firmly implanted in your mind: there is a place in God's heart that only you [I] can fill.

2005-2006. When we were covered up with family funerals: my mother-in-law, a cousin who died young, my sister-in-law, my father-in-law, my mother. Through all these losses I knew God was with us and helping us through it.

During the Day

If any hint of being cast down comes today, or in the days ahead, pull out one of those memories of knowing God's presence and love, and let it set you on track again. Let it rekindle the vision of who you are—a friend of God.

DAY SIX

In but Not of the World

"If you belonged to the world, it would love you as its own. As it is, you do not belong to the world, but I have chosen you out of the world."

—JOHN 15:19

Therefore, I urge you, brothers and sisters, in view of God's mercy, to offer your bodies as a living sacrifice, holy and pleasing to God—this is your true and proper worship. Do not conform to the pattern of this world, but be transformed by the renewing of your mind. Then you will be able to test and approve what God's will is—his good, pleasing and perfect will.

—ROMANS 12:1–2

Individual Christians and the church have never been able consistently to understand what it means to be "in the world but not of the world." Scripture is full of references and images to the fact that we are engaged in a struggle. Paul called it a war: "For we are not contending against flesh and blood, but against the principalities, against the powers, against the world rulers of this present darkness, against the spiritual hosts of wickedness in the heavenly places" (Eph. 6:12 RSV). Because we are in this war, we must not "conform to the pattern of this world, but be transformed by the renewing of your mind" (Rom. 12:2).

Jesus warned His disciples to be mindful of this: "If the world hates you, keep in mind that it hated me first" (John 15:18). It is easy to conclude that we are to be a missionary community in the world, committed to witnessing and serving in a way that will attract and invite other followers. From Jesus and Paul, this seems to mean that we, as Christ-followers, are to become a community of aliens who are in, but not of, the world.

In September of 1997, there was a groundbreaking service for a Roman Catholic cathedral to be constructed in Los Angeles. The Diocese of Los Angeles had commissioned the famous Spanish architect José Rafael Moneo to design the building. Their hope was that the cathedral, to be completed by the beginning of the millennium, would be a peculiar witness to the glory of God.

There were models of the cathedral at the groundbreaking service, and on the basis of the models, a Los Angeles reporter wrote a review of the cathedral. This is a part of what the reporter said: "Moneo is creating an alternate world to the everyday world that surrounds the cathedral, a testimony to the grandeur of the human spirit, an antidote to a world that is increasingly spiritually empty."

Then he wrote this sentence: "The cathedral, set in the midst of the secular city, will be an enclave of resistance."[1]

What an image . . . the church, an enclave of resistance. "Resident aliens" is a good term to describe this aspect of the nature of the church. Jesus Himself provided the model. He was fully in the world, but He lived by a contrasting set of realities and was always in tension with the world—and to a marked degree, always in resistance to it.

As the church, we've known in every period of our history that the very nature of the church provokes some form of resistance. There's always a sense in which kingdom ideals are in conflict with the world in which the kingdom is set. This expresses itself in different ways. We have to be careful about the nature and focus of our resistance, of how we live as "aliens." We must not deceive ourselves into thinking that if we can get the right king on the throne—that is, if we can elect the right president, the right congress, the right governor— if we can put "our people" in places of political power, then we can win the battle. There can be no kingdom without a king, and the kingdom to which we are committed has only one King: Jesus.

Individual Christians and the church must think more in terms of transformation than of confrontation. We need to think more about *a long obedience in the same direction*, more than about a quick fix that might bring superficial change. Our task, as an enclave of resistance, is to subvert the callused, materialistic, secular, godless culture of which we are a part—to subvert that culture at its root by living as though we believe that we do not live by bread alone; that there is a kingdom reality of love in which all those things that are expressed in Romans 12 are operative. Our love is without hypocrisy. We abhor what is evil and we cling to what is good. In honor, we give preference to one another. We are able to rejoice in hope, but we are also able to be patient in tribulation. We attend to the needs of the saints and we give ourselves to hospitality. We bless those who persecute us, we rejoice with those who rejoice, and we weep with those who weep. We associate with the humble and we do not see ourselves as wise in our own opinion. We don't repay evil for evil; we seek to live peaceably with all people. We feed our enemies and give them drink—we don't confront evil with evil but we seek to overcome evil with good.

As resident aliens, our mission becomes incarnational. We take seriously the words of Jesus, "As the Father has sent me, I am sending you" (John 20:21).

Reflecting and Recording

There's always a sense in which kingdom ideals are in conflict with the world in which the kingdom is set. Do you believe this? In what ways do you see kingdom ideals most in conflict with the world?

The world says, "Let me see how I can take advantage of any situation to get more for ME." The church says, "What can I do to help make it better for everybody, and by so doing, show you Jesus."

Read again the description of our "resistant witness" from Romans 12. As you read, put an "X" over the descriptive phrases that you need most to work on in your own life.

Spend the rest of your time reflecting about how you are going to work on making those attributes more real in your life.

During the Day

Select a couple of those resistant witness descriptions that you marked above that you are going to work on expressing today and in the days ahead.

The Ultimate Test of Discipleship

"As the Father has loved me, so have I loved you. Now remain in my love. If you keep my commands, you will remain in my love, just as I have kept my Father's commands and remain in his love. I have told you this so that my joy may be in you and that your joy may be complete. My command is this: Love each other as I have loved you. Greater love has no one than this: to lay down one's life for one's friends. You are my friends if you do what I command."

—John 15:9–14

There is an unforgettable confrontation between Jesus and John the Baptist in Nikos Kazantzakis's *The Last Temptation of Christ.* Jesus and John are sitting high above the Jordan in the hollow of a rock, where they have been arguing all night long about what to do with the world. John's face is hard and decisive. In contrast, Jesus' face is hesitant and tame. His eyes are full of compassion.

"Isn't love enough?" [Jesus] asked.

"No," answered the Baptist [John] angrily. "The tree is rotten. God called to me and gave me the ax, which I then placed at the roots of the tree. I did my duty. Now you do yours: take the ax and strike!"

[Jesus replied,] "If I were fire, I would burn; if I were a woodcutter, I would strike. But I am a heart, and I love."[1]

This heart is seen vividly in Jesus' last intimate time with His disciples. When He talked to us about being His friends, He said, "Greater love has no one than this: to lay down one's life for one's friends." Then He added, "You are my friends if you do what I command" (John 15:13–14).

Love is the ultimate mark of discipleship, the dynamic of our partnership with Christ. The call is radical—not revenge or retribution, not "an eye for an eye, and a tooth for a tooth," but love.

On Day Five of Week Four I shared a testimony from Peter Storey. In his witness that day in Nairobi, he told story after story of the sign of Christ alive, living in us. One of those stories out of South Africa is a powerful witness to our partnership with Christ in love, in prayer, and in witness.

A young white man came and knelt at the Communion rail in worship at his church one day. In counseling afterward, the fellow told his story, and shared a crippling burden of guilt. He had been a policeman in Soweta. Racial conflict and violence had reached fever pitch. Blacks had been oppressed by the government system of apartheid, which included dreadful brutality that had become familiar across the world. Now they were rebelling in every way possible. There was a youth uprising in Soweta in 1976, in which this policeman was involved. Now the gospel had touched him and he had searched his soul; he wanted to be clean. In repentance, he accepted Christ and sought forgiveness.

Some months later, he was welcomed into membership of the Methodist church in Johannesburg. He knelt at the Communion rail to be confirmed. The bishop who confirmed him was black. It was a powerful visual symbol: the black hands of the bishop reached out to be laid upon the white hands of this man who had once been his oppressor. The voice that confirmed this white man in his pardon, in his forgiveness, in his acceptance, spoke with a rhythm of black Africa. The walls were down! Love had prevailed.

Peter Storey closed his witness by sharing the fact that in his church in Johannesburg, on the altar, there stands a candle. It's not an ordinary candle, but it's surrounded by a coil of barbed wire. They call it the amnesty candle. Every Sunday there comes a moment in the service when the Christians who are gathered pray for South Africa. They read the names of those they know who are in prison, and they commit themselves again to justice. Then they light the candle and suddenly in the middle of those cruel, imprisoning coils of barbed wire, a flame begins to burn, and those Christians remember the words of John: "The light shines in the darkness, and the darkness has not overcome it" (1:5).

John closed the fifteenth chapter of his gospel with Jesus' reminder that a servant is not greater than his master, and that persecution may be our lot. But no matter, Jesus said that He would send the Counselor, who would bear witness to Him—"And you also must testify" (John 15:27).

Our witness (testimony) is to an amazing truth: we have been chosen by Christ, we are His friends, and love is the ultimate mark of our discipleship.

Reflecting and Recording

The apartheid situation that plagued Africa for decades was more dramatic than most of us can imagine. In most of our communities there are situations of estrangement, expressions of hate, people and groups that are being marginalized, and people and situations that cry out for reconciliation and love. Take a long, honest look at your community. Who are those persons, and what groups are being shut out and marginalized? Name them here.

Is your church or community of faith aware of these issues? Are they engaged in a love response? If so, are you a part of that response? What might the church do to be a kingdom presence with these people and in these situations?

During the Day

Talk to some person who is a part of your community of faith (who is not sharing this journey) about the issue of being in but not of the world. Share your concern about people and situations in which you think the church should be involved.

GROUP MEETING FOR WEEK FIVE

• INTRODUCTION •

John Wesley urged Christians to use all the means of grace available for their Christian walk—their growth in Christlikeness. We usually think of prayer, Scripture, study, worship, and Holy Communion when we think of growth practices. Wesley added Christian conferencing to this list. By this, he meant intentional Christian conversation—talking about spiritual matters and sharing our Christian walk.

These group sessions provide practice in the art of Christian conferencing. As you share together in the safe setting of a group of mutually committed persons, you are being equipped to share in less safe relationships. Keep this in mind as you share in this session and as you continue your weekly gatherings.

• SHARING TOGETHER •

1. You have finished five weeks of this workbook journey. Spend a few minutes talking about the experience in general terms. What is giving you difficulty? What is providing the most meaning?

2. Spend ten to fifteen minutes talking about Paul's two great concepts of the Christian faith: justification by grace through faith and the indwelling Christ. How much attention has been given to these concepts? Have you heard and thought enough about the *indwelling Christ* to think of it as a primary aspect of your own experience?

3. In sharing your own Christian experience, how much emphasis do you put on conversion ("justification") and how much on Christ in you ("the indwelling Christ")?

4. Invite someone to read the paragraph on page 118 beginning, "Stanley Jones made the observation . . ." then spend ten minutes discussing these claims.

5. Spend some time talking about judgment. Is our judgment implicit in our actions or failures to act? Is *abiding in Christ,* or *apart from Christ* the alternatives that determine our judgment?

6. Discuss the claim, "You will enjoy your discipleship in proportion to your obedience." Call for witnesses to verify this is true.

7. Spend the remainder of your time discussing *love* as the ultimate test of discipleship

• PRAYING TOGETHER •

There is a sense in which these weekly sharing sessions are actually prayer meetings. When we are together in Jesus' name, Jesus is there. We listen to others in love. We share, believing that we can be honest because we are loved and are gathered in the name and the spirit of Jesus. So there is a sense in which, throughout your sharing, you have already been corporately praying.

1. Leaders, read these words from Jesus aloud to the group: "I will not leave you desolate. I will come to you . . . and he who loves me will be loved by the Father . . . and the Father and I will come and make our home with him." Invite the group to sit silently for two minutes listening to Jesus say this to them.

2. Leader, remind the group that as they have shared together during the meeting, they have been praying, but as previously indicated, there is power in a community on a common journey praying together. Call each person's name, pausing briefly after each name for some person in the group to offer a brief verbal prayer, focused on what that person has shared. It could be as simple as, "Lord, thank You for Jane's testimony about her relationship with Jesus," or "for Jane's conviction that she is forgiven and is loved by Jesus." Make sure that everyone's name is called, including the leader, and that each person is prayed for, even if some who are more comfortable praying aloud prays for more than one person.

   When all names have been called and persons prayed for, sit in silence for two minutes. Be open to the strength and love that is ours in community.

God's Continuing Advocacy

Pentecost

When the day of Pentecost came, they were all together in one place. Suddenly a sound like the blowing of a violent wind came from heaven and filled the whole house where they were sitting. They saw what seemed to be tongues of fire that separated and came to rest on each of them. All of them were filled with the Holy Spirit and began to speak in other tongues as the Spirit enabled them.

—Acts 2:1–4

We've come in our time with Jesus in the upper room to what is recorded in John 16. In this chapter, Jesus talked a great deal about the work of the Holy Spirit. Jesus knew that the disciples were becoming increasingly aware of the certainty of His coming death. He was going away, and would no longer be with them. They were overwhelmed with sorrow, so He talked to them more about the Holy Spirit, the coming Helper, or Advocate.

Physically, He was going away, but their movement would not be stopped by His death. Instead, by His resurrected and living Spirit, He would be with them. Just as the incarnation had been evidence of God's forbearing love for the world, so would the coming of the Spirit be a sign of God's continuing presence and power. God was not giving up on humankind. Instead, by His Spirit, He would continue to manifest His presence and power in the world.

The fulfillment of that promise came on the day of Pentecost. According to the Gospels and the book of Acts, for forty days the resurrected Jesus appeared to His disciples and then ascended into heaven. But on the Jewish festival day of Pentecost, fifty days after Easter, we are told the Holy Spirit of God came upon the disciples in the city of Jerusalem.

Unusual phenomena occurred: the sound of a mighty rushing wind, what appeared to be tongues of fire rested upon the disciples' heads, and the ability to understand one another even though they spoke a variety of languages. Peter and the apostles said that this event was in fulfillment of the prophecies of Joel, the prophet, who said that in the latter days God would pour out His Spirit upon His people. Moreover, it was also the fulfillment of the promise of Jesus that after He departed from them, He would send His Spirit to them to be their Helper and Advocate.

As a result of the coming of the Holy Spirit on Pentecost, the Christian church was born. Peter preached the first gospel sermon about the divine significance of Jesus' death and resurrection. This one whom a sinful age had crucified, God had made both Lord and Christ by His resurrection from the dead.

Now, said Peter, God was beginning a new humanity with Jesus Christ at the head. Thus, the coming of His Spirit is the assurance that God has not given up on humankind. Instead, by His Spirit, He intends to be our Advocate, our Counselor, and Helper.

Reflecting and Recording

Spend a few minutes reflecting. How much thought do you give to the Holy Spirit? What role does the Holy Spirit play in your understanding of the Christian faith? In what ways have you experienced the Holy Spirit?

During the Day

Engage someone in a conversation about the Holy Spirit. Ask them the kind of questions you have been reflecting on.

Persecution? Maybe Not, But . . .

"All this I have told you so that you will not fall away. They will put you out of the synagogue; in fact, the time is coming when anyone who kills you will think they are offering a service to God. They will do such things because they have not known the Father or me. I have told you this, so that when their time comes you will remember that I warned you about them. I did not tell you this from the beginning because I was with you, but now I am going to him who sent me. None of you asks me, 'Where are you going?' Rather, you are filled with grief because I have said these things."

—John 16:1–6

Jesus was reflecting, maybe thinking to Himself, *What have I been saying to My friends? Have they heard Me rightly? Do they still not know what I'm talking about? How are they going to respond to what I have been saying?* So He decided He'd better say something about why He had said what He had said.

He minced no words. Danger was coming! There may be a time "when anyone who kills you will think they are offering a service to God" (v. 2).

Jesus wanted His disciples to know they will suffer. He talked specifically about His way and teaching, which brought conflict with the leaders of the synagogue. The disciples were going to be persecuted for their acceptance of Jesus' teaching and for following Him.

There are people today who are persecuted for their faith, some who are killed for following Jesus. That kind of persecution has not come to us . . . yet; it may be coming. We need to cultivate the presence and power of the Holy Spirit to endure whatever comes.

Jesus wanted His disciples to know that their suffering is not from the Father or Him. This raises the general question: Is God responsible for our suffering?

My Methodist preacher friend Norman Neaves did his clinical training in the chaplain's office at Duke University Hospital. He recalled an experience that put this discussion in stark reality.

Early in his training, a woman in the obstetrics ward requested that a chaplain come and offer a prayer of thanksgiving for the birth of her child. As he went to perform that pastoral task, he thought how wonderful it was that this mother wanted to offer such an act of thanksgiving. As he entered the room he was delighted to see her husband and her little six-year-old daughter there as well. They all joined hands together and Norman offered a prayer of thanksgiving to God for the birth of that beautiful little baby.

Later that same day, Norman received another call from the same ward. It was the nurse who wanted to talk to him, so he went back up the stairs again, sat down in the conference room, and the nurse told him a story that jolted him to the core. In that Room 418, where he had offered a prayer of thanksgiving for that healthy baby, behind the curtain in another bed in the same room, therefore able to hear everything that went on, was another mother who had a baby the same night. Yet her baby was born without arms and legs, some of its organs outside the body, and it wasn't expected to live.

The nurse said, "When you thanked God for the baby that was healthy and beautiful, the other woman began to cry. She had to bury her face in the pillow to keep from being heard. She began to wonder why God had done this terrible thing to her and sent her a grotesque baby, not even expected to live. Chaplain Neaves," the nurse said, "she's still crying, and we don't know what to do. I think you need to go and see her."

He was speechless. He didn't know what to say. He made his way to that woman's room and sat at her side. "I'm sorry," he said softly as he took her hand. "God didn't do this to you. He doesn't want anyone to come into the world maimed and deformed. I don't understand it, but I can't believe it's the will of God." Then he added, "You know, maybe God is crying now, too. Maybe out there in the great somewhere, He's shedding tears just like you and me. Maybe His heart is as broken as your heart and mine . . ."

I've had a lot of tough pastoral issues with which to deal, but none quite so stark in contrast and in the way this happened. I love to think I might have responded as sensitively.

His was the most appropriate and the most truthful response one could make, because that's really the way it is.

Somewhere along the way, we have to reshape our whole understanding of God. Sometimes it takes tragedy to force us to look more carefully and think more deeply, but also, to accept the mystery of God's activity in a world that has fallen, filled with events far astray from His will and desires for His children.

Our efforts to understand tragedy have to involve the fact that our all-powerful God has deliberately limited Himself out of love and gives us freedom. So this God is not the one who causes everything to happen, but the one who suffers, who experiences pain with us, who loves and cares about what happens to us.

Reflecting and Recording

How would you have responded to the woman who had given birth to the distortedly developed baby? Could the chaplain have added anything that would have been helpful?

I don't think he could have done any better. I, for one, can't imagine myself doing as well.

Recall an experience of suffering when you wrestled with how God might be involved. Make some notes to get it clearly in mind.

When Rebekah lost the quads. I didn't wrestle so much with how God might be involved as with finding how to console my husband, who couldn't get past being angry at God and rejecting Him for letting it

How did others seek to interpret that experience for you? Did you or they accredit the *happen.* suffering to God? If you felt God was responsible, how did you feel about God's action?

The ones around me, wisely, only expressed their sorrow for our sorrow and their love for us. All I could feel was the hurt and the helplessness of not being able to heal my children's heart.

During the Day

If you know someone who is suffering and may be tempted to blame God for the suffering, call them or write them a note, simply saying that you don't understand and that there is mystery in suffering, but you want to assure the person of your love and God's love.

The Holy Spirit Convicts

"But very truly I tell you, it is for your good that I am going away. Unless I go away, the Advocate will not come to you; but if I go, I will send him to you. When he comes, he will prove the world to be in the wrong about sin and righteousness and judgment: about sin, because people do not believe in me; about righteousness, because I am going to the Father, where you can see me no longer; and about judgment, because the prince of this world now stands condemned."

—JOHN 16:7–11

Jesus had been trying to comfort His disciples. Their eyes had been dimmed by their sorrowful hearts; they were seeing only that which affected them. All they felt was a sense of loss and desolation. Jesus' words must have been hard to even hear, much less consider. "It is to your good that I go away" (v. 7, author's paraphrase). How could that be?

He explains that staggering statement by what He had already expressed more than once: the Comforter, another Advocate, is going to come.

The King James Version expresses verse 7: "It is expedient for you that I go away: for if I go not away, the Comforter will not come." The word "expedient" suggests that which is done for practical or prudential reasons. Modern translations left that word behind, indicating that Jesus was not just explaining some practical issue, He was sharing the positive that was going to result in His going away. The Spirit was going to come, and His coming was going to be good. He was going to prove the world to be in the wrong about sin. Other translations have it "convict" or "convince" the world concerning sin, righteousness, and judgment.

There is a sense in which the outstanding first characteristic of the whole gospel message is the new gravity attached to the fact of sin—the inwardness, the universality, the awful destructiveness of it; the way it affects our whole being and all our relationship with God.

The beastly, destructive nature of sin cannot be fully conveyed by our human effort; the Spirit must do this essential work.

And it is essential. Alexander Maclaren has expressed this forcibly:

Everything in our conception of the gospel of Jesus Christ and of His work for us depends upon what we think about this primary fact of man's condition, that he is a sinful man. The root of all heresy lies there. Every error that has led away from Jesus Christ and His Cross may be traced to defective notions of sin and a defective realization of it. If I do not feel as the Bible would have me feel, that I am a sinful man, I shall think differently of Jesus Christ and of my need of Him, and of what He is to me.[1]

John Wesley believed that certain aspects of the Christian faith required special emphasis. Methodists today still hold to these emphases. There is no more simple or indeed better way of presenting these distinctive emphases than by using the four statements that collectively are called the "Four Alls."

1. All people need to be saved.
2. All people can be saved.
3. All people can know they are saved.
4. All people can be saved to the uttermost.

The first statement, all people need to be saved, is reflective of the biblical analysis of the human condition that all men and women are sinners having fallen "short of the glory of God" (Rom. 3:23). Like Martin Luther at the time of the Reformation, Wesley's sense of his own sinfulness gave a sharp focus to his theology. He was consumed with a passion for holiness and a living relationship with God. He could not produce any relief from his consciousness of sin, or any sense of fellowship with God by his effort at strict moral living, and a life of ruthless religious discipline could not produce any relief from the conscious-ness of sin. Even a period of missionary endeavor in Georgia served only to increase his feelings of alienation from God. As he wrote in his journal toward the end of that period: "This, then, I have learned in the ends of the earth—that I am fallen short of the glory of God . . . and having nothing in or of myself to plead, I have no hope . . ."[2]

Wesley insisted that all of humankind was in this position and wholly incapable of being delivered by human effort. Everyone needs to be saved from sin and its consequences; there is nothing anyone can do to save him or herself.

The Holy Spirit penetrates the innermost reaches of our own hearts to expose this fact of sin and our helplessness in escaping it. The Holy Spirit works in specific ways, revealing our obsessive materialism, our compulsive drive to succeed at any cost, our pride that keeps asserting our self-worth before God and robs us of saving relationships, our sensuality that turns others into sex objects to satisfy our lust, our holding on and hoarding to feed our appetite for security.

Paul declared that the Holy Spirit "searches everything" (1 Cor. 2:10 RSV). Maybe we wish that the Spirit were not quite so nosy, but it's for our own good.

The living Spirit of Christ reminds us of our sin and witnesses to us of our worth in God's sight. God loves us so much that He died on the cross to save us from destruction and death.

Reflecting and Recording

Since the Holy Spirit is central to the gospel and to the core of our living the Christian life, we need to pray more to and for the Holy Spirit. One of Isaac Watts's hymns, "Come, Holy Spirit, Heavenly Dove," is a powerful prayer.

Come, Holy Spirit, heavenly Dove,
With all Thy quick'ning powers;
Kindle a flame of sacred love
In these cold hearts of ours.

Look how we grovel here below,
Fond of these trifling toys;
Our souls can neither fly nor go
To reach eternal joys.

In vain we tune our formal songs,
In vain we strive to rise;
Hosannas languish on our tongues,
And our devotion dies.

Dear Lord! and shall we ever live
At this poor dying rate?
Our love so faint, so cold to Thee,
And Thine to us so great!

Come, Holy Spirit, heavenly Dove,
With all Thy quick'ning powers;
Come shed abroad the Savior's love
And that shall kindle ours.

Read the hymn reflectively as a prayer.

Now, focus on stanza two: "Look how we grovel here below, Fond of these trifling toys." Are there suggestions here for particular sins the Holy Spirit might want to remind you of?

Careless speech, worrying about finances, most of all, weak and timid witness.

During the Day

Memorize or copy the first stanza of the hymn. Carry it with you or place it in a place where you will be reminded to pray it often during the day.

DAY FOUR

The Holy Spirit Guides

"I have much more to say to you, more than you can now hear. But when he, the Spirit of truth, comes, he will guide you into all the truth. He will not speak on his own; he will speak only what he hears, and he will tell you what is yet to come. He will glorify me because it is from me that he will receive what he will make known to you. All that belongs to the Father is mine. That is why I said the Spirit will receive from me what he will make known to you. . . . Very truly I tell you, you will weep and mourn while the world rejoices. You will grieve, but your grief will turn to joy. A woman giving birth to a child has pain because her time has come; but when her baby is born she forgets the anguish because of her joy that a child is born into the world. So with you: Now is your time of grief, but I will see you again and you will rejoice, and no one will take away your joy. In that day you will no longer ask me anything. Very truly I tell you, my Father will give you whatever you ask in my name. Until now you have not asked for anything in my name. Ask and you will receive, and your joy will be complete."

—John 16:12–15, 20–24

As Christians, we are not left to grope in the dark. Jesus said in verse 13, "But when he, the Spirit of truth, comes, he will guide you into all truth." That's a primary work of the Holy Spirit. He lives within as our personal guide. Romans 8:14 says, "For those who are led by the Spirit of God are the children of God."

In a broad sense, the Holy Spirit has two ministries, one to the sinner and one to the saint. Yesterday, we considered His ministry, convicting and convincing us of our sin. That begins before we enter the Christian life. In fact, the explicit beginning of the Christian life is when we are so convicted of our sin that we repent; through faith, accept the grace of Christ; and accept Him as Savior and Lord.

That work of "convicting of sin" does not cease then; it goes on in our life as we abide in Christ and seek to reflect His life in the world. Yet, generally, we can say that the Holy Spirit has two ministries, one to sinners and one to saints.

Jesus wanted His disciples to know that the Holy Spirit would be their guide, and would guide them particularly in *all truth*. Truth is the major concern of the Holy Spirit. In fact, both here in John 16:13 and in John 14:17, He is called "the Spirit of truth."

Are you listening? The Holy Spirit guides us to receive the truth.

Jesus knew and acknowledged there was a lot of truth the disciples needed to learn, to record, and pass on to us. But at that particular moment they were not ready for it. "I have much more to say to you, more than you can now bear" (John 16:12). Those first years following Jesus' death, resurrection, and ascension were critical. The church was called into being, shaped, and empowered by the Holy Spirit; the gospel spread; the life, teaching, ministry, death, and resurrection of Jesus was recorded; and, along with letters written to the churches and messages received from the Spirit by apostolic leaders, the New Testament came to be.

The Holy Spirit guided all that. He came to guide us into the truth that really matters and that truth is found in the Bible. We do not understand the truth in the Bible apart from the work of the Holy Spirit.

The apostle Paul said in 1 Corinthians 2:12, "What we have received is not the spirit of the world, but the Spirit who is from God, so that we may understand what God has freely given us." We have received the Spirit of God, that He might enable us to receive the truth of God. John promised, "He will glorify me because it is from me that he will receive what he will make known to you. All that belongs to the Father is mine. That is why I said the Spirit will receive from me what he will make known to you" (John 16:14–15).

Anybody can read the Bible without the help of the Holy Spirit, but it is impossible to truly understand the Bible apart from the Holy Spirit. Not only does the Holy Spirit reveal the truth, He leads and empowers us to respond to the truth.

God's Word is demanding; responding is no casual or easy matter. We must discipline ourselves in study and reflection on God's Word, but there is a difference in knowing and obeying.

Acts 13:2 is an extremely revealing verse: "While they were worshiping the Lord and fasting, the Holy Spirit said, 'Set apart for me Barnabas and Saul for the work to which I have called them.'" Did you note that? The Holy Spirit spoke as they "were worshiping the Lord." If you only have a walk with Jesus on Sunday, don't expect to hear from the Spirit on Monday. But if you will take time everyday to minister to the Lord, to get into the Word, to speak with the Lord, you'll hear from the Lord and the Spirit will guide you.

The Holy Spirit is not an independent contractor. He does not speak on His own. When He speaks, He speaks what He hears from the Father and the Son.

The Holy Spirit will never lead you into any area or situation that will violate the Word of God. That's why we know that the Holy Spirit never leads a Christian to marry a non-Christian. For 2 Corinthians 6:14 says, "Do not be yoked together with unbelievers." That's why we know that the Holy Spirit would never lead a church to ordain a practicing homosexual or, for that matter, a practicing adulterer to the ministry. The Word of God makes it plain that the practice of homosexuality and adultery are sins, and the Holy Spirit, neither by reason nor by emotion, will ever lead you in such a way as to cause you to run head-on into the Word of God

The problem with most believers is not that we need guidance in what we don't know, it is that we are not obeying what we do know. The way to learn the will of God in an unknown area of your life is to obey the will of God in the known area of your life.

The Holy Spirit will lead you to receive truth, and He will lead you to remember truth only if you are already determined to allow Him to lead you to respond to the truth.

Reflecting and Recording

Are you wrestling with an issue for which you need guidance? Name that issue here.

Have you shared this struggle with a person you trust? Have your prayed for the Holy Spirit's guidance? Are you obeying what you already know about that issue? If the Holy Spirit guides you in relation to the issue, will you obey His guidance?

During the Day

Continue using the hymn from yesterday:

Come, Holy Spirit, heavenly Dove,
With all Thy quick'ning powers;
Kindle a flame of sacred love
In these cold hearts of ours.

DAY FIVE

God Hears

". . . Now is your time of grief, but I will see you again and you will rejoice, and no one will take away your joy. In that day you will no longer ask me anything. Very truly I tell you, my Father will give you whatever you ask in my name. Until now you have not asked for anything in my name. Ask and you will receive, and your joy will be complete."

—John 16:22–24

Prayer is the exercise through which Christ's presence and power is appropriated. Jesus wants us to realize this so He expresses it twice in this brief passage.

This is a dramatic and powerful affirmation about prayer, and there are powerful implications. The first is simple, but difficult for us to stay convinced of: God hears us when we pray. Simple as it is, it's not always easy to appropriate or to really believe.

Many readers will know the name Edward R. Murrow, a pioneer in broadcasting. With smooth, solemn tones, he became the dean of broadcasters during World War II. He died much too young, a victim of lung cancer. He was never seen without a cigarette in his hand.

Clarence Forsberg tells about some people who were influential in Murrow's life; one was a woman named Ida Lou Anderson. They met at Washington State University. He was a student, and she was on the faculty, but they were the same age. He had stayed out of school a number of years, working in order to save money. Ida Lou was just out of college and in her first teaching appointment. She was a polio victim and had been in a wheelchair since she was nine years old. It was a strange relationship—this rough and ready young man, not as poised and suave as he would become, fresh out of the woods in the Pacific Northwest, and the frail young woman in the wheelchair. But there was a special rapport. Somehow he discovered that he could talk to her and she would listen.

Some years later when Murrow was about to be married, he wrote to his fiancée about Ida Lou.

> She's very much a part of my life and always will be, in a way that is hard to understand. She taught me to love good books, good music, gave me the only sense of values I have, caused me to stop drinking myself to death. In letters, I have talked over with her every decision that I have made. She knows me better than any person in the world. The part of me that is decent, that wants to do something, be something, is the part she created. She taught me to speak. I owe the ability to love to her, and to her you owe the things you like in me.[1]

Reflecting on that, Forsberg asked Murrow how she did it.

> She did it by listening. All of us need somebody who will listen. We need somebody who will hear us. They may not tell us what we want to hear, and they may not be able to do what we ask them to do. The important thing is that whatever we need to say, they are willing to listen.[2]

That's what prayer is all about. God hears you. You can tell Him exactly what is on your heart, and He will listen.

Reflecting and Recording

Is there a person in your life whom you trust to listen and hear you? If so, call that person today and thank them for the important role they play in your life. If they have time, tell them the story of Edward R. Murrow; it will make them feel good about the role they are playing.

Spend a few minutes, asking yourself, *Am I a good listener? If not, why?*

If you believe that God hears and listens, what are the three most important things you would like to tell God today?

1. Thank you for all the blessings you have already given me, and all those to come.

2. Thank you especially for the man you have given me to spend my life with. Guide me so that I may be a true blessing to him and show him your love.

During the Day

3. Keep him safe until the day he fully accepts and understands that love for himself, and let me live to see it. Thank you for bringing us this far together.

We shared previously that if we abide in Christ, and Christ indwells us, then we communicate Christ in our relationships. As you relate to others today, listen and hear, knowing that the Christ in you is listening and hearing.

God Cares

"In that day you will ask in my name. I am not saying that I will ask the Father on your behalf. No, the Father himself loves you because you have loved me and have believed that I came from God. I came from the Father and entered the world; now I am leaving the world and going back to the Father."

—John 16:26–28

For this is what the Lord says: "I will extend peace to her like a river, and the wealth of nations like a flooding stream; you will nurse and be carried on her arm and dandled on her knees. As a mother comforts her child, so will I comfort you; and you will be comforted over Jerusalem."

When you see this, your heart will rejoice and you will flourish like grass.

—Isaiah 66:12–14

Yesterday we considered the fact that a foundational truth about prayer is that God hears. A second truth we need to underscore is that God cares what happens to you. Jesus made sure His disciples knew they were loved by the Father. In different ways He continued to tell them that *the Father Himself loved them*.

There are all sorts of images, symbols, metaphors, and similes we can use to talk about God. And every term we use is limited; no image is complete. All the metaphors and figures that we use to portray God's personality—to color God's character—to reveal God's relationship to us—all of them apply, but none of them can be taken singly.

Scripture provides some beautiful expressions of God being like a mother. Johnstone G. Patrick reminds us, "[T]he Scriptures . . . speak to us with many voices, but never more persuasively than when . . . they sound forth the maternal note of the Eternal One."[1] In Deuteronomy, God is seen like an eagle stirring *her* nest: "As an eagle stirreth up her nest, fluttereth over her young, spreadeth abroad her wings, taketh them, beareth them on her wings" (32:11 KJV).

This verse comes from the song Moses sang for Israel when he was an old man. The exodus was nearing an end and Joshua had been commissioned to take God's wanderers into the Promised Land. Moses looked back over that unforgettable journey with God, which had begun with a flaming bush, and he sang about how God had dealt with them, and he used the fluttering wings of an eagle to make his point.

Johnstone G. Patrick wrote:

Maybe out in the wild ways of Midian, one fine morning, Moses had watched a great mother eagle hovering over and around her nest, trying to tempt her fledgling to take off for the first time into the broad upper air. But the little fellow, not knowing yet what eagle wings were for, refused to leave the comfortable nest on the craggy ledge. Then the mother bird rose in the air above and with a sudden swoop struck the nest and the young bird and sent them hurtling out into space. The fledgling was forced to fly now, and around him the mother eagle flew, till at last the young bird's strength gave out. At once the mother swept swiftly beneath, and took her offspring on her outstretched wings, where for a short while he rested and regained his strength.[2]

The picture here of the eagle forcing her young from the nest is the image of a mother who cares enough for her young that she dislodges them from their secure nest in order that they may do what they were born to do—to soar on eagle's wings.

What a precious picture! When the young one is weary and can fly no longer, the mother swoops beneath him and on her own wings bears him up.

Look at the second picture of the Mother God, from Matthew's Gospel. Jesus was weeping over Jerusalem because they had not accepted the Messiah who had come to save them. You can feel the anguish and pain in His voice as he said, "O Jerusalem, Jerusalem

. . . how often I have longed to gather your children together, as a hen gathers her chicks under her wings, and you were not willing" (Matt. 23:37).

You may have to be from rural Mississippi, or from some farm background to really know how graphic this image is. How often have I seen a mother hen do exactly what Jesus suggested He wanted to do for Jerusalem. I've seen the old hawk soaring overhead, doing his surveillance, spotting the hen and her little chicks. And I've seen that very sensitive mother hen—I don't know whether she hears the hawk or sees the hawk—but she senses danger. She knows what is about to happen. She gives that mother "cluck-cluck-cluck" and the little biddies hover around and she protects them beneath her wings. The hawk is not to be outdone. He soars down and attacks the mother hen, but she fights him off. He comes again, and she fights him off. Courageously, with all the energy that is hers, she does it even though her head and her body is bloodied.

It's a graphic picture of the protecting love of a mother hen, and Jesus said that's what He wanted to do for Jerusalem. He wanted to gather the children of Jerusalem unto Himself as a hen would gather her brood.

It's a rewarding exercise to reflect on the method of the mother eagle and the mother hen. The mother eagle suggests something of severity—pushing the little ones from their nest—but the mother hen suggests courageous goodness. And don't we know from Scripture that that is the nature of God—the severity and goodness of God—His sovereignty, and yet His oneness with us? In the eagle, there is a suggestion of loftiness; in the hen, there is the suggestion of lowliness. "Majesty and meekness meet together in the motherhood of God, and severity and goodness are reconciled."[3]

And now another final picture: God is like a mother providing the comfort that only a mother can provide. Isaiah reported God, saying, "As one whom his mother comforts, so I will comfort you; you shall be comforted in Jerusalem" (Isa. 66:13 RSV).

How very human, and how very descriptive and picturesque. Earlier Isaiah said: "For you will nurse and be satisfied" (v. 11). Is there a more characteristic picture of love than a mother tenderly nursing her child? It is an iconic picture of the comfort and caring of our Mother God.

Some years ago the great Christian Rufus Jones was devastated by the sudden death of his young son. The staggering blow left him in the depths of despair. One day while out for a walk, he came to a beautiful estate. He saw a little girl, about five or six years old, come running out an iron gate. She closed the gate behind her, but suddenly realized she had locked herself out. She began to cry and beat on the gate hysterically. Quickly, her mother came running to the little girl, opened the gate, took the little girl in her arms, carried her back inside, and comforted her saying, "Everything is all right, Honey. You know I wouldn't leave you out here all alone. You know how much I love you. You knew I would come, didn't you?"

As Rufus Jones saw that young mother coming to rescue her daughter, he remembered that God is like that . . . and no matter what the situation is, even at the place of death, He is there for us. Jones said, "In that moment, I saw with my spirit that there was love behind my shut gate also."

Reflecting and Recording

Our primary focus today has been on the metaphor of God as a Mother. Spend a bit of time thinking about that. Is it a new image for you? In what way is it helpful or unhelpful for you to think in that fashion?

List the three most common images you use in thinking about God.

Which of those images is your favorite? Write a brief prayer, addressing God with that image, thanking God for listening to and caring for you.

During the Day

In our thinking these past few days, we have centered on the fact that God is good, God cares, and communication with God is possible. These are foundational principles of prayer. Believing this, find a few quiet minutes at different times during the day and simply talk to God about what's important to you.

DAY SEVEN

We Shall Overcome

"Do you now believe?" Jesus replied. "A time is coming and in fact has come when you will be scattered, each to your own home. You will leave me all alone. Yet I am not alone, for my Father is with me.

"I have told you these things, so that in me you may have peace. In this world you will have trouble. But take heart! I have overcome the world."

—John 16:31–33

A number of translations introduce that last verse differently: Be of good cheer! Cheer up! . . . Never lose heart! . . . Be brave! . . . I have overcome the world! Our good news is this: because Christ has overcome, we shall overcome!

Two of the things that my wife, Jerry, and I like to do together is going to estate sales and auctions. We don't buy very much, but we have a good time. It's one of the most relaxing things we do.

Occasionally we come across a real treasure. We recently did that one Saturday afternoon, at an estate sale. It cost me only fifty cents. It's a book by Mother Teresa of Calcutta called *Life in the Spirit*. Mother Teresa is one of my heroes. I have a number of her books and a number of books about her in my library, but I didn't have this one. I was excited.

I began reading it as soon as I returned home, and I came across this meditation that speaks to the notion of overcoming. It said:

Remember that the passion of Christ ends always in the joy of the Resurrection of Christ. So when you feel in your heart the suffering of Christ, remember the

Resurrection has to come—the joy of Easter has to dawn. Never let anything so fill you with sorrow as to make you forget the joy of the Risen Christ.[1]

That's the perspective we need to keep: the perspective that we will not be free of trouble and pain and difficulty; that will never be the case. Jesus made that clear: "In the world you have tribulation" (John 16:33 RSV). The perspective is not that we will be free of trouble, pain, and difficulty, but that we will overcome.

A family in our church has experienced this firsthand, and profoundly, during the past few months. Tom shared his story at our men's prayer breakfast, and gave me permission to share it here.

For several long, long months, Tom has been without a job. It has been a trying time, and to a marked degree, a test—a test not only for him, but for his wife, and their two teenage children.

Throughout this time, both Tom and his wife have been convincing witnesses to the sustaining power of prayer, and to patience as a gift of the Spirit. Only once or twice during these long months did I detect a dreariness of spirit on Tom's part, a waning of confidence.

At what must have been one of those low times, the subject came up at the dinner table. In the conversation, Tom expressed his anxiety: "I don't know when I'm going to get another job. I'm beginning to wonder if I ever will."

After some silence, as that thought pervaded, their seventeen-year-old son Kevin responded, "Dad, don't worry, the Big Man doesn't shaft His sheep."

That may not be the way you would express it. Our language is not always as clear. But we don't miss the truth—and Tom got it. Christ is our Shepherd, and He's not going to shaft His sheep. He's not going to cut us loose, or abandon, or forget us.

We know; we have experienced the truth of it: "In the world [we] have tribulation." But Jesus' word is, "Be of good cheer [take heart], I have overcome the world" (John 16:33 RSV).

In the novel *Patience of a Saint,* Andrew Greeley has a character named Red Kane. He is a rough, hard-living reporter in Chicago. Then he undergoes a dramatic conversion experience, which he describes as "being zapped by God." But after this impactful spiritual breakthrough, instead of things getting better for him, they go from bad to worse. His family turns from him. He loses his job. A novel he writes is rejected. Frustrated and disgusted with what he considers being let down by God, he goes to his pastor and seeks assurance that God is going to reward him for changing the direction of his life. But the pastor is honest and tells him: "The Lord offers no guarantees. Your novel may be rejected again . . . you may not find another job and reconciliation with your family may take a long time."

Afraid he might lose everything, Red Kane says to himself: "If God expects that kind of courage from anyone, then God should provide some guarantees."[2]

Well, He does, but not the kind of guarantee most of us wish for. The guarantee is not a money-backed one, but a life-backed one. We will not be free of trouble, difficulty, and pain, but we will overcome. We can count on it. "In this world you will have trouble. But take heart! I have overcome the world" (John 16:33). We can count on overcoming the world.

The last verse of Horatio Spafford's hymn "It Is Well with My Soul" says it with verse:

And, Lord, haste the day when the faith shall be sight,
the clouds be rolled back as a scroll;
the trump shall resound, and the Lord shall descend,
even so, it is well with my soul. (author's emphasis)

The gift of prayer is that God hears and God cares what happens to us. Because Christ has overcome, we shall overcome.

Reflecting and Recording

The hymn writer prayed, "Lord, haste the day when the faith shall be sight." Express that prayer in your own words here.

Are you going through some trouble now for which the outcome is not yet seen, but you have faith? Rest for a minute or two, believing Jesus' promise, "In me you may have peace" (John 16:33).

During the Day

Do you know a person who is going through some tribulation for which the outcome is not yet seen? Find a way today to encourage faith in that person. Maybe share your own experience and this promise of Jesus.

GROUP MEETING FOR WEEK SIX

• INTRODUCTION •

You are drawing to a close of this workbook venture. You have only one more planned group meeting. Your group may want to discuss future plans. Would the group like to stay together and pursue another study? Are there resources (books, tapes, periodicals) that the group would wish to use corporately? Would two or three of you like to provide leadership and offer this journey to some others you would personally invite?

Being a part of a group requires responsible participation. Some of us, in a group setting, feel the temptation to play it safe and not risk being honest and vulnerable. This is even true about such positive issues as forgiveness and joy.

Energy is another issue. Listening and speaking demand physical, as well as, emotional energy. The temptation is to hold back, to be only half present, not to invest the attention and focus essential for full participation. I urge you to withstand these temptations. These sharing sessions are very important. Don't underestimate the value of each person's contribution.

• SHARING TOGETHER •

1. Spend twenty to thirty minutes sharing the most important insight each person has received this week. Don't just name the insight; talk about its meaning in your life, how it came about, and why you think it was important for you this week. What is going on in your life to make this insight or lesson important?
2. Invite a couple of people to share an experience of suffering in which they wrestled with how God might be involved.
3. The hymn printed in the Reflecting and Recording section on Day Three is a good expression of the work of the Holy Spirit. Have someone read that hymn aloud to the

group, then spend ten minutes identifying and discussing different expressions of the Holy Spirit's working.

4. Invite a person or two to share an experience of being guided by the Holy Spirit.

5. Spend five to ten minutes discussing the image of God caring like a mother. Are you bothered by the image when our primary image of God is Father? How is the image a helpful one for you?

• PRAYING TOGETHER •

1. Invite the group to share concerns and needs, especially the need for Holy Spirit guidance that may have been named in your Reflecting and Recording on Day Four. Have a season of open corporate prayer, inviting as many people as will to offer brief prayers in response to what has been shared.

2. Close your time together by praying aloud the prayer to the Holy Spirit printed on Day Three.

Listening to Jesus Pray

Prayer Is a Revealing Picture of the Person Praying

After Jesus said this, he looked toward heaven and prayed: "Father, the hour has come. Glorify your Son, that your Son may glorify you. For you granted him authority over all people that he might give eternal life to all those you have given him."

—JOHN 17:1–2

Prayer is a revealing picture of the person praying. Here, in John 17, we have a picture of Jesus. He has been talking to His friends, now He talks to His Father. It has been called "the High Priestly Prayer" because here our High Priest intercedes for us and His church. He pours out His love and thoughts and concerns to His Father and He lifts us to God's throne of grace where there is mercy and pardon.

We have reflected on prayer during this journey of listening to Jesus, but here in John 17, we have the opportunity of hearing Jesus pray.

Nothing reveals more of who a person is than the content of his prayers. Dom Hélder Câmara, until retirement, was the archbishop of Olinda e Recife in North-East Brazil, the least-developed part of the country. He has been the incarnation of the best of liberation theology, making real in his own life that God has taken a preferential option on behalf of the poor. He was short in stature, but a giant spiritually and in commitment. His unrelenting struggle for people to be able to live together as brothers and sisters has its roots in, and is empowered by, an intimate communion with Christ, a disciplined life of prayer.

Since he was in seminary, he has made it a practice to get up at about 2:00 a.m. In the silent darkness he listens and speaks, and that is prayer. He listens for and hears the voices daytime noises tend to drown. God speaks, nature speaks, his deepest self speaks, and he hears the voice of the poor and oppressed, as well as the oppressors, and the apathetic.

During those early hours he has written thousands of brief reflections, the heart of his prayers. José de Broucker collected these for a book called *A Thousand Reasons for Living*.

In these pregnant expressions we listen to a giant pray. The very first entry in the book tells us who Dom Helder is.

> I wish I were
> a humble puddle
> that would reflect the sky.[1]

My temptation is to record a number of these pungent spiritual gems; one other helps paint his portrait.

> On the bare wall
> Was left a single nail
> for a picture which had gone.
>
> Are more needed
> to prompt me to pray,
> When three nails support
> the Redeemer of the world.[2]

Prayer is a revealing picture of the person praying.

Reflecting and Recording

Live for a brief time with the first entry of Dom Helder. In the space by his entry, make some notes describing this man as you see him through his prayer. What was he like? What must have been some of his characteristics? In your mind, does Dom Helder look a lot like Jesus? How much like Jesus are you?

During the Day

Pay attention to the people with whom you interact today. How much like "I wish I were a humble puddle" are any of them? What about you?

Jesus' Understanding of Himself

"I have brought you glory on earth by finishing the work you gave me to do. And now, Father, glorify me in your presence with the glory I had with you before the world began."

—JOHN 17:4–5

This entire prayer is spoken out of the living union that Jesus had with the Father throughout eternity. It must have given Jesus a great sense of mission accomplished to say that His disciples "know in truth that I came from thee" (v. 8 RSV). Yet, the intensity of His prayer continues, "that they all may be one; even as thou, Father, art in me, and I in thee" (v. 21 RSV).

This is Christianity's unique claim: the incarnation. God has come to us in Jesus Christ.

Let me put it in contrast. There are few men in the twentieth century who seemed as immortal as Mao Tse-Tung. Chairman Mao became the incarnation of a movement, a system of thought, and a revolution that impacted the entire population of China (900 million people at the time). He lived to be eighty-three, and was China's leader for more than three decades. It was difficult for even the most casual observers to imagine China without Mao, yet he died.

An admirer wrote shortly after Mao's death: "He conceived of the Chinese Revolution, and then helped cause it to happen, and in the process, the thought of Chairman Mao became the primary thought of every Chinese. The word almost literally became flesh."[1]

Notice the conditional word: *almost*; the word almost became flesh.

John, writing of Jesus, said: "The Word became flesh" (John 1:14). No reservation, no conditional definition!

I was in China two years after Mao's death. His likeness in picture and statue was still everywhere, yet, the mausoleum built to keep his body as a glorious reminder, was closed. The official word was that it was closed for repair, but a guide whispered to me that it was the government's effort to diminish the place of Mao in the thought and culture of China. That diminishing work has continued.

It is obvious that Chairman Mao will take his place in history with other great shapers of national life, but the limitation is still there. In Mao, powerful man that he was, the word almost became flesh; but in Jesus, the Word became flesh. "The Word became flesh and made his dwelling among us. We have seen his glory, the glory of the one and only Son, who came from the Father, full of grace and truth" (John 1:14).

This is the incredibility of the incarnation. Jesus Christ is God in flesh.

Reflecting and Recording

Back in 1866, Benjamin Handy wrote a hymn called "Who Is He in Yonder Stall?" that is known by too few and sung too little in our congregations. The first stanza asks, "Who is he in yonder stall at whose feet the shepherds fall?" The chorus answers, "'Tis the Lord, O wondrous story! 'Tis the Lord, the King of Glory."

This is a succinct expression of the incarnation, yet not a complete picture. In the balance of the hymn, Handy completes the picture in this series of questions:

Lo, at midnight who is he who prays in dark Gethsemane?
Who is he in Calvary's throes asks for blessings on his foes?
Who is he that from the grave come to heal and help and save?
Who is he that from your throne rules the world of light alone?

After each question the answer in the hymn comes in the chorus, "'Tis the Lord, O wondrous story! 'Tis the Lord, the King of Glory."

Get your favorite picture of Jesus in your mind. Keep that picture vivid there as you spend time now, reflecting on the incarnation and who we are paying attention to in these last hours of His life.

During the Day

Carry that picture of Jesus with you throughout the day, rehearsing who He is by remembering how Handy portrayed Him in his hymn: "'Tis the Lord, O wondrous story! 'Tis the Lord, the King of Glory."

I Have Manifested Your Name

"I have manifested thy name to the men whom thou gavest me out of the world;
thine they were, and thou gavest them to me, and they have kept thy word. Now they
know that everything that thou hast given me is from thee; for I have given them the
words which thou gavest me, and they have received them and know in truth . . . that
thou didst send me."

—John 17:6–8 RSV

Jesus put it in what may at first sound quaint: "I have manifested thy name." It is a
powerful word about Jesus' self-understanding. It is also a revelation of Jesus' mission
and who God is.

In Jewish thought, name is used in a very special way. The psalmist said, "They that
know thy name will put their trust in thee" (Ps. 9:10 KJV). Name does not simply mean what
a person is called, it means the nature and character of the person as far as it can be known.

From the time of Moses, the Israelites knew God as Yahweh, the great "I Am." But the
time came when the name of God was so sacred that it was never spoken, except by the
High Priest once each year on the Day of Atonement, alone in the Holy of Holies. The name
was so sacred that Jews were afraid to sound it, even in worship, so the name of God was
not spoken.

Then Jesus came. The silence was broken. "I have manifested thy name." Other translations have it, "I have made thy name known" (TEV), or "I have revealed you," or "I have
spelled out your character in detail" (MSG).

Reuben Welch reminds us that Jesus came,

not only knowing the name of God but bearing the name of God . . . He became the ultimate revelation of God to His people.

In Old Testament times, God instructed His people to worship at the place where He put His name, at the tabernacle and later the temple. Jesus' own person replaced the tabernacle/temple. He fulfilled the promise of God's presence; He became the place where we meet God. He is the place where God has put His name.[1]

The poet Edwin Markham put it succinctly:

Here is truth in a little creed,
enough for all the roads we go:
in love is all the law we need,
in Christ the only God we know.[2]

Unless we get this, we will miss the power of the gospel. If we don't begin here, our thought journey about God will be like a wilderness wandering. Jesus is God's gift of salvation and eternal life. He is God's promise that we don't have to go it alone. We are not left as orphans; God is with us.

Jim Harnish in his book *What Will You Do with King Jesus*? tells a haunting, tragic story. After his father's death, a fellow confided with Jim that he would remember his father primarily as a man balancing himself on top of a huge mound of ice. The mountain raised him above other people, but at the same time, it trapped him. Whenever he would consider the possibility of coming down off his perch, one look at the slippery-ness of the slope would discourage him. Furthermore, if he did come off that mountain, he would be just like everyone else, sharing their weakness and their humanity. He lived his life up there, isolated from human relationships, praying that the dark would keep his mountain intact, cursing the sunlight of human love which kept trying to melt it all away.[3]

Jesus has come to tell us that God is not like that. In fact, our God is like Jesus who wept when people rejected His love, saying, "How often I have longed to gather your children together, as a hen gathers her chicks under her wings, and you were not willing" (Matt. 23:37).

So Jesus prayed, "I have manifested thy name" (John 17:6), and now we know that name is Love.

He also said, "I have brought you glory . . . by finishing the work you gave me to do" (John 17:4). Was Jesus anticipating the cross? The work God had given Christ to do was the work of salvation. "For God so loved the world that he gave his only Son, that whoever believes in him should not perish but have eternal life" (John 3:16 RSV). The foundation work of salvation was the cross.

William Barclay, in his commentary on Christ finishing the work God gave him to do (John 17:6), told the story of a famous painting from the First World War. It showed an engineer fixing an essential field telephone line. He had just completed the line so that the messages might come through, when he was shot. The painting shows him in the moment of death, and beneath it there is one word, *Through*!

He had died, he had given his life, that the message might get *through*. That is exactly what Jesus did. He had completed His task; He had brought God's love to men. For Him that meant the cross; and the cross was His glory because He had finished the work God gave Him to do; He had made men forever certain of the love of God.[4]

Reflecting and Recording

Look seriously at the following assertions and reflect for a moment after each and ask, *Am I claiming who Jesus is in my faith and witness?*

Jesus is God's gift of salvation and eternal life.

Jesus is God's promise that we don't have to go it alone.

We are not left as orphans; God is with us.

During the Day

Find a way today to share with someone these three affirmations about Jesus.

What Jesus Thinks of Us

"I am coming to you now, but I say these things while I am still in the world, so that they may have the full measure of my joy within them. I have given them your word and the world has hated them, for they are not of the world any more than I am of the world. My prayer is not that you take them out of the world but that you protect them from the evil one.

"They are not of the world, even as I am not of it."

—John 17:13–16

In His prayer Jesus not only tells us about the nature of God, we learn what Jesus thinks of us. He makes it clear that we must live our lives in Him, but also in the world. He is not only consecrating us to Himself, He is consecrating us for the world. We are to be in the world what He has been for the world.

On Day One, we had a brief introduction to Dom Hélder Câmara's reflections. One of those reflections pictures clearly our being in Christ and in the world.

This puffy
dirty face,
stained with sweat,
bruised by falls
or blows,
belongs to some beggar or drunkard?

Or are we perhaps on Calvary
gazing at the holy face
of the Son of God . . . ?[1]

As Jesus is God's instrument of our salvation, we must be in the world as those who have received salvation, sharing it with others.

D. T. Niles understood this and talked about evangelism in this fashion:

Evangelism is witness. It is one beggar telling another beggar where to find bread. A Christian does not offer out of his bounty. He has no bounty. He is simply a guest at his Master's table and, as evangelist, he calls others too. The Christian stands alongside the non-Christian and points to the gospel, the holy action of God. It is not his knowledge of God that he shares, it is to God Himself that he points. The Christian gospel is the Word become flesh. This is more than and other than the Word become speech. The religious quest for self-realization is henceforth pulled up with this demand, that the self is not realized by a flight from the finite and the temporal, but by taking its stand at the point where the finite and the infinite, the temporal and the eternal meet.[2]

What an awesome call, to be in the world as Christ's presence and witness, to realize our self by taking our stand at the point where the temporal and eternal meet!

But there is more. Jesus commissions us to be in the world *for* Him, but He insists that we are not *of* the world, so He prayed, "Sanctify them by the truth; your word is truth. As you sent me into the world, I have sent them into the world. For them I sanctify myself, that they too may be truly sanctified" (John 17:17–19).

Jesus' prayer is that His followers are to be *for* Him *in* the world. They are to be holy; that's what "sanctify" means. To be holy is to be set apart, to be different because we belong to God.

A story going around is of the young man who was converted one spring. His friends worried about him going off to work that summer in a lumber camp. They felt that the rough, tough worldly lumberjacks might tease him harshly, and perhaps tempt him to let go of his faith. So they prayed for him daily.

When the summer was over, the young man came back home. "What was it like?" his friends wanted to know. "Did you make it okay? Did the lumberjacks give you a hard time because of your faith?"

He responded, "Oh, there weren't any problems at all. They never found out I was a Christian."

Unfortunately, that's the way it is with too many of us. Our faith never shows. Somewhere I saw a placard that read, "If you were ever arrested for being a Christian, would there be enough evidence to convict you?"

To be sure, only God is holy in separateness, purity, righteousness, and wholeness. We become holy in our relationship with Him. When Jesus prayed that the Father "sanctify us in the truth," He is praying that our time, talent, energy, attitudes, intentions—all that we are—is marked with the sign of consecration. An overwhelming thought, impossible to imagine except by the promise He gives us: "For them I sanctify myself, that they too may be truly sanctified" (v. 19). It is not something we can achieve; the power of Christ Himself is available to us. We become holy as we allow Christ to live in us, as we live our lives for God, not for the world.

For many years, George Balanchine was the director of the New York City Ballet, and a legend in the world of dance. To members of that New York troupe, "Mr. B" was not only the director, he was the audience. The dancers danced only for Mr. B. If he was not pleased, the applause of the audience meant little.

It must be so with us. Christ is our director and audience. We live our lives for Him.

Reflecting and Recording

Spend a few minutes reflecting on this statement: As Jesus is God's instrument of our salvation, as those who have received salvation, we must be God's instrument by sharing His salvation with others.

In what way do others identify you as a Christian?

In what way might others consider you holy?

During the Day

Live today knowing that you may be the only Christ someone will see.

Jesus Prays for the Church

"My prayer is not for them alone. I pray also for those who will believe in me through their message, that all of them may be one, Father, just as you are in me and I am in you. May they also be in us so that the world may believe that you have sent me. I have given them the glory that you gave me, that they may be one as we are one—I in them and you in me—so that they may be brought to complete unity. Then the world will know that you sent me and have loved them even as you have loved me.

"Father, I want those you have given me to be with me where I am, and to see my glory, the glory you have given me because you loved me before the creation of the world.

"Righteous Father, though the world does not know you, I know you, and they know that you have sent me. I have made you known to them, and will continue to make you known in order that the love you have for me may be in them and that I myself may be in them."

—John 17:20–26

Jesus prayed not just for those who are gathered with Him there in the upper room, but for those who would believe in Him "through their word" (v. 20 KJV), and those who would be with Him forever. What an expansive prayer! This is a prayer for the church that is going to be born as a resurrection people; us today, and those of future generations who believe in Him.

Jesus prayed that these believers will be one in knowing the glory and love of the Father, and sharing that experience with the world.

The purpose of the church is "that the world may believe that you have sent me" (v. 21) and that the world may know that "you have loved them even as you have loved me" (v. 23).

What an awesome task and privilege! Through the witness of forgiven sinners, the world will know forgiveness. Through the love of people who know themselves loved (though undeserving), the world will know God's love. Sir Edwyn Hoskyns stated clearly this radical nature of the church: "What the Incarnate Son of God had once been to Jewish people, the Church is now to the world, the incarnate love and glory of God."[1]

So a key phrase here is, "that the world may believe" (v. 21). What is required of us to make that happen?

One: involvement. Look again at verses 15 and 16: "My prayer is not that you take them out of the world but that you protect them from the evil one. They are not of the world, even as I am not of it."

We must not forget that it is in the turbulent world that we must live. The Christian life can never be a retreat from the world. Jesus did not pray that we would find a way to escape, but that we find victory. There may be a place for the monastery and the convent, but they can never be a model for the life to which Jesus calls us. A life withdrawn from the world is a distorted version of the Christian faith.

Two, integrity is an essential characteristic for Christians to lead the world to believe. This is closely akin to, if not one and the same, with holiness: Christians whose profession and performance are in harmony. Jesus prayed that we may be sanctified by the truth (see John 17:19). That's integrity.

In an issue of *Parables*, Jim Voras told of a national spelling contest in Washington, DC. In the fourth round of the contest, Rosalie Elliott, then an eleven-year-old from South Carolina, drew the word, *avowal.* In her soft, Southern accent, she spelled it. But did the seventh grader use an "a" or an "e" as the next to the last letter? The judges couldn't decide. For several minutes they listened to tape-recording playbacks, but the critical letter was accent-blurred. Chief Judge John Lloyd finally put the question to the only person who knew the answer. "Was the letter an 'a' or an 'e'?" he asked Rosalie.

Surrounded by whispering young spellers, she knew by now the correct spelling of the word. But without hesitating, she replied, "An 'e,'" acknowledging that she had misspelled it.

She walked off the stage. The entire audience stood and applauded, including fifty newspaper reporters, one of whom was heard to remark that Judge Lloyd had put quite a burden on an eleven-year-old. Rosalie rated a rousing affirmation, and it must have been a heart-warming and proud moment for her parents.[2]

It was a spelling bee, and eleven- and twelve-year-olds were the actors, but it's a forceful parable. The world will believe when our performance is in harmony with our profession, when they see Christians who will not cheat on their income tax, who will stand up for peace with justice, who will love even when it costs, who will stand with the poor and oppressed, believing Jesus, "Whatever you did for one of the least of these brothers and sisters of mine, you did for me" (Matt. 25:40). They will believe when they see Christians who will use their money as a gift from God to bless other's lives, who will use their money to guarantee that the gospel is preached all over the world, that health and wholeness are offered in Jesus' name.

The world will believe when it sees Christians who believe the Ten Commandments are not out of date, and the Sermon on the Mount is as relevant in our city today as it was in AD 35 in Galilee, and that the highest and the only principles that will save us and keep this world sane are those laid down by Jesus, all rooted in that ultimate principle: "Love one another. As I have loved you, so you must love one another" (John 13:34)

Integrity is the word . . . performance and profession in harmony, that the world may believe.

Reflecting and Recording

Looking back over your life, locate two or three times your integrity was tested both in terms of truth-telling and action. Briefly describe the testing and your response.

I was desperate to find a job. I went to an interview and was hired for a job that paid only $5 a week and turned out to be sales rather than writing. Then my employment agency called with a chance to interview for a job more in tune with my training, which would probably have paid much more. I told the agent I would not go for the other job because I had already given my word that I would take the low paying one. It didn't work out, but I had kept

Spend two or three minutes examining whether your daily performance is in harmony with your profession.

Not always. I am often careless in speech and respond to some situations with more anger than love. These are problems of mine that I am praying for help to overcome. With God's help I can do so.

During the Day

Order your day, remembering Jesus' word, "Whatever you did for one of the least of these brothers and sisters of mine, you did for me" (Matt. 25:40).

DAY SIX

The Sustaining Source

"Father, I want those you have given me to be with me where I am, and to see my glory, the glory you have given me because you loved me before the creation of the world.

"Righteous Father, though the world does not know you, I know you, and they know that you have sent me. I have made you known to them, and will continue to make you known in order that the love you have for me may be in them and that I myself may be in them."

—John 17:24–26

Jesus made it clear: we are to be those who guarantee that the world may believe. The question is: What sustains us in the critical work of witness and discipleship? Our cue is in verses 22 and 23: "That the glory which thou hast given me I have given to them . . . and thou in me, that they may become perfectly one, so that the world may know that thou hast sent me and hast loved them even as thou hast loved me" (RSV).

If these words sound a bit clumsy, the truth is this: Christ has given Himself to us that we may give ourselves to each other. "I in Thee, and Thou in Me," Jesus says to God. That's incarnation, but there's more. "That they may be one, even as we are one," takes it even further, and the word I would use for it is *interdependence*. Christ has given Himself to us that we may give ourselves to each other.

E. Stanley Jones expressed on numerous occasions the point of this final part of Jesus' prayer in his three-part sentence: "You belong to Christ; I belong to Christ; we belong to each other." Jesus is describing the oneness that comes when Christians share the experience of the presence and the glory of God in the lives of His people and in the world.

The pastor/scholar Earl Palmer said:

This is the first theological explanation in Scripture of the mission of the Christian in the world. The Christian strategy is not portrayed in terms of rugged individualism. This is a community enterprise. There are no apostolic heroes who will be so brave and so strong that they will be able to make it alone in the world. As they supremely need Jesus Christ, they will also need each other. Note the relational development. As Christ gives to them the gift of the Holy Spirit to abide in them and with them on the journey, so now he gives them each other. This means that the strategy in the world is to a people—a holy colony—real people in a real place, set down in the midst of the wavy line of history. This colony of men and women will experience and know the Word became flesh—"and these know that thou hast sent me" . . . . This means that as Christians together experience the reality of the love of Christ, then the world is drawn to consider the meaning of God's love."[1]

Incarnation and interdependence: Christ has given Himself to us that we may give ourselves to each other. This is what sustains those who would be the guarantee that the world may believe.

Reflecting and Recording

Spend some time examining your life and ponder this question: Who are those Christ has given you with whom you share and with whom you are making a witness of Christ's presence?

Arc you accepting the gift of others in relationship? Are you doing your share in giving yourself to and in relationship?

During the Day

Be attentive to all the people you interact with today. To whom might you say, "You belong to Christ; I belong to Christ; we belong to each other"?

Eternal Life

After Jesus said this, he looked toward heaven and prayed:

"Father, the hour has come. Glorify your Son, that your Son may glorify you. For you granted him authority over all people that he might give eternal life to all those you have given him. Now this is eternal life: that they know you, the only true God, and Jesus Christ, whom you have sent."

—John 17:1–3

This week we have concentrated on the prayer of Jesus in His last evening with His disciples. I chose not to deal with these verses in the order of the text because the beginning of His prayer in verses 1–3 are not only pivotal words in the prayer, but in these five chapters we have been studying.

The resounding word of the gospel and Christian experience is that Jesus Christ is alive, alive forevermore and, hopefully, alive in you and me. Jesus exclaimed, "This is eternal life: that they know you, the only true God, and Jesus Christ, whom you have sent" (v. 3).

"I have made you known to them," He prayed (v. 26). This is no new message from Jesus. It is His prayer that what He had taught would become a reality. Remember His beautiful metaphor in John 15 of the vine and the branches, in which He tells us who He is in relation to God and who we are in relation to Him. "Abide in me, and I in you. As the branch cannot bear fruit by itself, unless it abides in the vine, neither can you, unless you abide in me. I am the vine, you are the branches. He who abides in me, and I in him, he it is who bears much fruit, for apart from me you can do nothing" (vv. 4–5 RSV).

That invitation of Christ, "abide in me," and our response to the invitation became the primary concern of Paul. He prayed for the Ephesians and us, "that Christ may dwell in your hearts through faith; that you, being rooted and grounded in love, may have power to comprehend with all the saints what is the breadth and length and height and depth, and to know the love of Christ which surpasses knowledge, that you may be filled with all the fullness of God" (Eph. 3:17–19 RSV).

Wow! Difficult to even think about. "That you may be filled with all the fullness of God" (v. 19). Philips translates that: "May you be filled through all your being with God himself!" And the New English Bible has it: "So may you attain to fullness of being, the fullness of God himself."

As fantastic as it is to ponder, that's at the very core of the Christian faith: Jesus Christ, alive, and wanting to live in us.

"And this is eternal life, that they know thee the only true God, and Jesus Christ whom thou hast sent" (John 17:3 RSV) is not the only way Jesus stated His promise. He said, "Because I live, you will live also" (John 14:19 RSV). And even more dramatically and specifically, "I am the resurrection and the life: he that believeth in me, though he were dead, yet shall he live" (John 11:25 KJV). There are two ways of looking at this, or maybe it's just two sides of the same coin. One is the promise of resurrection *now*: "this is eternal life." That's present tense. And when Jesus said, "Because I live, you will live also," that's also present tense.

When we look at it this way, the proof of the resurrection is not the empty tomb, but the incredible transformation in the lives of the disciples, which is a matter of record. They remained ordinary men after the resurrection, but they began to live extraordinary lives.

Something had happened to them. As my mother down in Mississippi would say, "something had come over them"; they were living the resurrection *now*.

There is the other side of the coin, Jesus' soul-bracing promise, "I am the resurrection and the life: he that believeth in me, though he were dead, yet shall he live" (John 11:25 KJV). This is the promise of eternal life beyond death.

In the first week of this venture, I shared about the baptism of the granddaughter of my dearest friend, Buford Dickinson. He had died and was not physically present for the marriage of his daughter and the baptism of her first child. Buford was my dearest friend and his death was a painful blow. In my grieving, John Birkbeck, my Scot Presbyterian preacher friend and spiritual mentor, gave me this beautiful word: "For the Christian, death is not a period in the written sentence of life, but a comma, for eternal life is our gift." So it is; death is not a period, but a comma.

Later, my friend John died on Thursday of Holy Week, and we all knew how he would celebrate dying three days before Easter. He was eighty and very sick. Fluid around his heart made it almost impossible to breathe. Our letter exchanges through the years had been a great source of joy and strength for me. I still miss that, but I'll carry with me forever the memory of our last three hours together. The December before he died, I was in a meeting in London, and left the meeting a day early to fly north to Aberdeen, Scotland, where John lived in retirement. I felt this would be our last time together on earth.

He couldn't get out of bed, so we spent our three hours in his upstairs bedroom. The taxi came and it was time to go. I read from Romans 8: Nothing can "separate us from the love of God," then I prayed. The taxi driver blew his horn, but I refused to be rushed. I hugged him, and through tears said clumsily, "I'll see you, John." He lifted his frail hand . . . and it was shaking as he held it high and pointed heavenward . . . and in a loud rasping whisper, he said, "Tomorrow . . . tomorrow!"

I'm looking forward to that—tomorrow! My brother, Lloyd, who died too early, saving the life of two others; my preacher grandfather, Lewis Dunnam, whom I never knew; my dear friends, Buford and John—tomorrow!

Reflecting and Recording

Write some notes here about how you perceive living eternal life *now*.

Spend as much time as you have available now, looking back over this workbook journey listening to Jesus. Make some notes identifying highlights, new insights, challenges, and new directions for living a Christ-life in the world.

If you are part of a group sharing this journey listening to Jesus, prepare to share some of these notes in your closing group session.

During the Day

Find someone today to share the fact that you have been on this seven-week journey, and invite them to read chapters 13–17 of John's Gospel in the fashion that you have been reading it, as Jesus' last message to us.

GROUP MEETING FOR WEEK SEVEN

• INTRODUCTION •

This is the last meeting designed for this group. You may have talked about the possibility of continuing to meet. If so, conclude those discussions and plan how to move forward with your decisions. Whatever you choose to do, it is usually helpful to determine the actual timeline in order that participants can make a clear commitment. Assign a couple of people to follow through with whatever decisions are made.

Your sharing during this session should reflect the entire seven-week experience. (Leaders: save enough time to respond to suggestion 6. Begin with your workbook experience this week.)

1. Invite someone to read Edwin Markham's poem on Day Three, then spend fifteen to twenty minutes discussing the incarnation, beginning with responding to the last line of the poem, "In Christ the Only God We Know."
2. In His prayer, Jesus made the claim to the Father, "I have manifested your name." As those who are *in Christ,* what would it mean for us to manifest His name?
3. Spend some talking about how others might identify you as a Christian.
4. "You belong to Christ; I belong to Christ; we belong to each other." Discuss how these three claims of Stanley Jones are related.
5. Spend ten minutes sharing with one another how you perceive living eternal life now.
6. Spend the remainder of your time sharing what these seven weeks have meant to each participant—new insights, challenges, and things they need to work on in their lives.

• PRAYING TOGETHER •

1. Begin your time of prayer by inviting as many persons as will to briefly express gratitude to God for something significant that happened to them as a result of these seven weeks.

2. Give each person an opportunity to share whatever decision or commitment he or she has made, or will make as a result of listening to Christ during these seven weeks. After the sharing, invite two or three persons to offer prayers of thanksgiving and support.

3. A benediction is a blessing or greeting shared with another, or by a group, in parting. The "passing of the peace" is such a benediction. Close your time together in a benediction of the love and power of Jesus. Have your group get into a circle. The leader will begin the benediction, holding the hands and looking into the eyes of the persons to his or her right, saying, "The love and power of Jesus go with you." The person will respond, "and also with you," then turn to the person to his or her right and exchange the same greeting. Be sure that the leader receives that blessing from the person to his or her left when the blessing goes around the circle.

4. Having completed the passing of the blessing of the love and power of Jesus, speak to one another in more spontaneous ways. Move about to different persons in the group, saying whatever you feel is appropriate for your parting blessing to each person. In your own unique way, bless each person who has shared this journey with you.

NOTES

Week One, Day One

1. E. V. Rieu, *The Word: The Bible from 26 Translations* (Gulfport, MS: Mathis Publishers, Inc., 1988), 2099.

Week One, Day Seven

1. Keith Green, "Rushing Wind," *The Keith Green Collection* (1981), Sony/ATV Music Publishing LLC.

Week Two, Day Six

1. Bruce A. Demarest, *Who Is Jesus? Further Reflections on Jesus Christ: The God-Man* (Eugene, OR: Wipf & Stock Publishers, 2007), 102.

Week Three, Day Two

1. Alexander Maclaren, *Expositions of Holy Scripture, Vol. 10* (Grand Rapids, MI: Baker Books, 1982), 203.

Group Meeting for Week Three

1. *The Book of Common Prayer,* 334, The Collect at the Prayers of the People, #2, 394.

Week Four, Day Three

1. Robert Morgan, *On This Day in Christian History: 365 Amazing and Inspiring Stories about Saints, Martyrs and Heroes* (Nashville, TN: Thomas Nelson, 1997).

Week Four, Day Five

1. Proceedings of the 15th World Methodist Conference in Nairobi, Kenya, on July 23–29, 1986, edited by Joe Hale, 173–74.

Week Four, Day Seven

1. William Barclay, *The Gospel of John, Vol. 2, The New Daily Study Bible* (Edinburgh: Saint Andrews Press, 2001), 208–9.

Week Five, Day One

1. E. Stanley Jones, *In Christ* (Nashville, TN: Abingdon Press, 1961), 101–7.

Week Five, Day Four

1. G. K. Chesterton, edited with introduction and notes by Craig M. Kibler, *Orthodoxy* (Lenoir, NC: Reformation Press, 2002), 230.

Week Five, Day Five

1. William Barclay, *The Gospel of John, Vol. 2, The New Daily Study Bible* (Louisville, KY: Westminster John Knox Press, 2001), 208.
2. Ibid.

Week Five, Day Six

1. Mark Trotter, "An Enclave of Resistance," sermon, First United Methodist Church, San Diego, California, October 5, 1997.

Week Five, Day Seven

1. Nikos Kazantzakis, *The Last Temptation of Christ* (New York: Simon & Schuster, 1998 repr.), 241.

Week Six, Day Three

1. Alexander Maclaren, *Expositions of Holy Scripture, Vol. 11, St. John, Chaps. XV to XXI* (Grand Rapids, MI: Baker Book House, 1982), 96.
2. Richard Watson, *The Life of the Rev. John Wesley* (Nashville, TN: Southern Methodist Publishing House, 1857), 57.

Week Six, Day Five

1. Clarence J. Forsberg, "What You Need to Know about Prayer," sermon, Missouri United Methodist Church in Columbia, Missouri, on January 26, 1986.
2. Ibid.

Week Six, Day Six

1. Johnstone G. Patrick, "God, the Mother," *The Pulpit*, May 1963, 13.
2. Ibid., 14.
3. Ibid., 15.

Week Six, Day Seven

1. Mother Teresa, *Life in the Spirit: Reflections, Meditations, Prayers*, ed. Kathryn Spink (New York, NY: Harper & Row Publishers, 1983), 63.
2. Quoted by Donald Shelby, "God Is God," sermon, First United Methodist Church, Santa Monica, CA, June 26, 1988.

Week Seven, Day One

1. Dom Helder Câmara, ed. José de Broucker, *A Thousand Reasons for Living* (London: Docton, Langman and Todd, 1981), 19.
2. Ibid., 34.

Week Seven, Day Two

1. Orville Schell, *In the People's Republic: An American's First-Hand View of Living and Working in China* (New York: Random House, 1977), viii.

Week Seven, Day Three

1. Reuben R. Welch, *Let's Listen to Jesus* (Wilmore, KY: Francis Asbury Press, 1985), 67.
2. Edwin Markham, "A Creed," www.poetryexplorer.net.
3. James A. Harnish, *What Will You Do with King Jesus?* (Nashville, TN: The Upper Room, 1987), 90.
4. William Barclay, *The Gospel of John, Vol. 2, The New Daily Study Bible* (Edinburgh: Saint Andrews Press, 2001), 241.

Week Seven, Day Four

1. Dom Helder Câmara, ed. José de Broucker, *A Thousand Reasons for Living* (London: Docton, Langman and Todd, 1981), 97.
2. D. T. Niles, *That They May Have Life* (New York: Harper and Brothers, 1951), 96.

Week Seven, Day Five

1. *The Fourth Gospel*, ed. R. N. Davey (London: Faber and Faber, Ltd. 1947), 502.
2. Quoted by Don Shelby, "Who's in Charge Here?" sermon, First United Methodist Church, Santa Monica, CA, September 16, 1984.

Week Seven, Day Six

1. Earl F. Palmer, *The Intimate Gospel* (Waco, TX: Word Books, 1978), 146.